GEN Z
GRADUATES TO
ADULTHOOD

Recommendations From The Oldest Members of Generation Z For Marketers & Employers And Insights On Societal Issues And Aspirations

MARK BEAL
Foreword By Alyssa Rivers

Published by Mark Beal Media, LLC.

Toms River, New Jersey

Cover Design: Nura Hill

ISBN: 9798802026038

First Printing: 2022 Printed in the United States of America

Gen Z Graduates To Adulthood: Recommendations From The Oldest Members of Generation Z For Marketers & Employers And Insights On Societal Issues And Aspirations is available for bulk orders, special promotions and premiums. For details, all Mark Beal at +1.848.992.0391 or email markbeal@markbealmedia.com

To my wife, Michele, thank you for consistently encouraging me to pursue my passions for more than 30 years and to live life to the fullest.

To my Gen Z students, past and present, and my Gen Z mentees, thank you for welcoming me into your world and culture. You have inspired me with your entrepreneurial mindset, your purposeful approach and your innovation in transforming and challenging the status quo.

To the hundreds of professionals in my network, thank you for taking time to guest lecture in one of my courses and collaborate with dozens of Gen Zers or meet one-on-one with my Gen Z students to offer career advice, an internship or even a full-time job as they graduate to adulthood. Your investment of your time, experience and knowledge in response to my request provided more value to a Gen Zer than you could ever imagine.

Acknowledgements

A book like this can't be written and published without the participation of more than 60 of the oldest members of Generation Z, ages 22-26, who are leading the way for the younger members of their generation. I first want to thank all the Gen Zers who took time to provide their insights on marketing, employment, societal issues and the future. They include Antonia A., Brian A., Alexis B., Danielle B., Layston B., Sam B., Sean Bo., Sean Bu., Brittany C., Carl C., Gianna C., Jenna C., Lara C., Lauren C., Margaret C., Ashley D., Jenna D., Jennifer D., Joelle D., Summer D., Troy D., Cristina F., Gabrielle F., Olivia F., Adam G., Katie G., Paris G., Pat G., Alessandra I., Ryan J., Gillian, K., Hannah, K., Kayla L., Kymani L., Micah L., Rachel, L., Hanalee M., Matilda M., Sarah M., Julianna N., Frankie P., Michael P., Sarah P., Alyssa R., Flor R., Kylie R., Roya R., Shelby R., Sydney R., Geno S., Hailley S., Isaiah S., Rebekah S., Ryan S., Samantha S., Isabeau T., Rachel U., David W., Nicole W., Oliver W., and Nicholas Y.

I want to thank Alyssa Rivers for writing the book's foreword. Alyssa was an outstanding student of mine at Rutgers University at the undergraduate and graduate levels. She represents all of my amazing Gen Z students who consistently inspire me. Alyssa embodies all that is great about Gen Z. She is an entrepreneur who is innovative in her approach and transformative in her thinking. She prioritizes diversity, inclusion and belonging, and is seeking that same focus from companies and organizations.

I want to thank all of my outstanding students, past and present. My current students inspire me each and every day. My past students are inspiring in how they lead and transform business and society.

I want to thank all of my colleagues at Rutgers University. They are a dream team of thought leaders, researchers and teachers.

I want to thank the awesome members of the student-run public relations agency at Rutgers University, Scarlet PR.

I want to thank Aneesh Dhawan and his innovative Gen Z research company, Knit, based in Austin, Texas. Knit is one of the few Gen Z-only research firms. Aneesh and Knit provided some of the Gen Z data points you will read in this book. Like Generation Z, Knit is innovative and transforming the way market research is conducted. My collaboration with Knit is another reason why I am so bullish on Gen Z.

I want to thank all of the public relations, marketing and communications professionals in my network who consistently take time out of their busy schedules to connect and collaborate with my Gen Z students whether in the classroom as a guest speaker or one-on-one as a mentor and advisor.

I want to thank members of the media who have always taken an interest in my books and content and shared with their followers including, but not limited to, Bob Considine, Gordon Deal, Michael Diamond, Mike Emanuel, Bruce Ferrell, Casey Freelove, Eileen Hoenigman Meyer, Michael Smith, Anthony Uva, Kevin Williams and many more.

I want to thank the professional associations and organizations that continuously share my Generation Z research and insights from my books with their members including, but not limited to, the Association of National Advertisers (ANA), American Marketing Association (AMA) especially the New Jersey chapter, Public Relations Society of America (PRSA), the Public Relations Student Society of America (PRSSA) especially the Todd Hunt Chapter at Rutgers University.

I want to thank Nura Hill for the time and expertise she invested in designing and publishing this book so that employers, marketers, media and educators will benefit for many years to come.

Last, but certainly not least, I want to thank my family.

I want to thank everyone in my family who inspires my research and writing and supports my passion projects including my wife Michele (Gen X), my son, Drew (Millennial), Drew's wife, Huda (Millennial), their son, Marc (Gen Alpha) and daughter Nadine (Gen Alpha), my daughter, Meghan (Millennial), and Meghan's son, Luke (Gen Alpha), and my daughter, Summer (Gen Z), and Summer's husband, Nick (Millennial), and their daughters, Mia (Gen Alpha), Aria (Gen Alpha) and Ava (Gen Alpha).

Contents

Foreword

By Alyssa Rivers

I was recently asked the question, "If you could go back and tell your high school self one thing, what would it be?" At the time, I said that I would give myself a break and that it would all work out in the end. As I sit here now at 23-years-old thinking about myself at 16 or 18, I would say that there are going to be some bumps in the road; that I'll graduate during a pandemic, but I will have met lifelong friends, that I'll go into college as an undecided major but come out with two degrees, a full-time job and a mentor who I continue to respect and admire to this day. Mark Beal has always been paramount in my educational and professional journey. From the moment I stepped into his Principles of Public Relations course in 2018 to being a smiling face at my Master of Communication and Media program graduation in 2021, Mark has been instrumental in helping me achieve my goals and further my career. For him, it's not about the praise or the accolades but the desire to help his students and a passion for bringing insights and new perspectives to educators and professionals through his books that will be crucial knowledge for years to come. It is for those reasons, that I am honored to write the foreword of *Gen Z Graduates To Adulthood: Recommendations From The Oldest Members of Generation Z For Marketers & Employers And Insights On Societal Issues And Aspirations,* for one of the greatest mentors and professors that I have had the pleasure to meet so far in life.

Mark's commitment to decoding this generation is beautifully depicted in *Gen Z Graduates To Adulthood,* as he outlines the challenges we have faced and the aspirations we have set for ourselves in the future. When I graduated in 2020 during the pandemic, everyone said that we were the class that was going to make a change. We'd been through something extremely difficult, and we would emerge resilient. As a member of Gen Z, I am in a constant state of limbo as I am not old enough to be a millennial but also don't identify with the youngest members of my generation. Regardless, being a Gen Zer means that we embody words such as creative, mindful, changemaker, authentic and innovative. We are a generation of individuals who saw the paradigm shift, as Mark alludes to in his work because we sit at the forefront of a transitional period in society. We're analyst, engineers, storytellers, content creators, environmentalists, social activists, medical professionals, lawyers, entrepreneurs, and quite frankly, anything we want to be. Gen Z cannot be categorized as one thing or perspective because we are not all the same, and oftentimes, marketers can forget that and craft campaigns that don't look at us individuals on a spectrum. To connect with us means to look at both sides as we range from age 10 to age 26 and realize that a one size fits all approach is no longer feasible like it had once been.

Uniquely, as a Gen Zer, I am at the forefront of culture, innovation, and the everchanging pace of the marketing world. We consume media in a whole new way because we've left traditional media behind and created our own content because we have learned the importance of what it means to be our own brand and use that to our advantage. My generation has a wealth of knowledge that marketers must tap into in order to excel in the future, so hire us, ask us questions, and don't be afraid to challenge the status quo...because we aren't. As Mark will discuss in later chapters, we do not consume media the way that millennials do, we take a purpose-driven approach to almost everything we do, and we are your most important consumers. The time has passed for traditional means of marketing and campaign building. We know we have much to learn from our peers and from the generations that precede us. However, we are proactive in gaining that knowledge in order to excel in our professional and personal lives. Want my advice? Be bold, take risks, stop thinking of us as selfish or lazy but rather driven and forward-thinking, and simply ask questions and I promise we'll give you an answer.

Gen Z Graduates To Adulthood is filled with brands that we identify with, causes that we support, advice for how to market to us, and most importantly, insights into what we want in life and the goals and ambitions that we aspire to obtain. Part III and IV explain that if you want to engage with us, you must learn our likes, our behaviors, and understand that the time to underestimate what we can bring to the workforce is over. Simply put, it's not enough to just be "cool" anymore. To be "cool" means to engage with celebrities who are multifaceted, ethical, and paving their own way in the world when you build marketing campaigns. It means to take a stand and support social issues in a genuine way because we are a generation of activists and influencers who want to be loyal to a brand that aligns with our beliefs. By the same token, *Gen Z Graduates To Adulthood* illustrates the importance of gaining our trust and creating an environment that not only lets us thrive but creates equal and collaborative spaces for everyone. Without doing this, history has shown how marketers and brands can be seriously impacted by a lack of cultural understanding and competence when brands don't take the time to do their research. Give us a seat at the table because we are intersectional in our race, sexuality, identity, gender, experiences and are open to having these conversations to improve your brand and marketing approach moving forward.

In the end, the advice offered in this book comes from over 60 survey participants who share the notion that we live in an incredibly diverse world, therefore, you will find Gen Zer's from all walks of life who have something to offer.

Hire them, take the time to listen to them, appreciate and engage with their perspectives and experiences. Start to dig into the brands that we align with such as Nike, Instagram, Netflix, and Patagonia, and ask yourself, "what is it that they're doing that is drawing this generation in?" and then begin to take those next steps. In the end, we can be your introduction into the way that society and marketing are beginning to shift, only if you're willing to give us a chance to show our hard work and talent. Gen Z has taken the leap and stepped out of the box, and we hope you'll join us.

ALYSSA RIVERS
Rutgers University Alumna, Class of 2020 & 2021

Introduction

In the fall of 2017, I had a lightbulb moment. I had just completed teaching a 300-level public relations course at Rutgers University that morning where I was inspired and energized by my collaboration with the students, mostly sophomores and juniors. As I drove to my office, I had an epiphany. I realized that while millennials had been the primary focus of many of the campaigns that me and my public relations agency colleagues had developed and executed over the previous decade for category leading consumer brands, Generation Z (Gen Z) would become the priority for corporations, brands and organizations of all sizes when the calendar turned to 2022 and beyond.

That singular moment of inspiration took me on an amazing journey that led me to immerse myself in the world and culture of Gen Z. For the past five years, my collaboration with members of Gen Z has resulted in this book, *Gen Z Graduates To Adulthood*, the third book that I have authored that focuses on those individuals who were born between 1997-2012. My Gen Z research has also led to invitations from leading organizations (Major League Baseball, Madison Square Garden Networks, Gannett, Kimberly Clark, Lab Corps, Prudential, Denny's, Big East Conference, National Lacrosse League, YMCA), trade associations (Association of National Advertisers, Public Relations Society of America, American Marketing Association) and conferences (New Jersey Digital Marketing Conference, Sport Techie) to present my Gen Z research, insights and implications in the form of keynote speeches and interactive workshops.

In 2018, I authored, *Decoding Gen Z*, which explored what Gen Z was doing on their mobile phones, their favorite social media channels and how they communicated. In 2020, I partnered with an innovative Gen Z student, Michael Pankowski, from Harvard University, and we co-authored, *Engaging Gen Z*. This book went beyond *Decoding Gen Z* and offered advice to employers, marketers and media companies regarding how to effectively engage this cohort that does not respond to traditional advertising, how to recruit and retain Gen Z employees who are seeking an innovative workplace culture and how to capture the attention of a generation whose media preferences are unprecedented.

In 2022, the oldest Gen Zers turn 25 and 26-years-old. Gen Z is no longer comprised exclusively of students which it was when I started my Gen Z immersion in 2017. Starting with the class of 2018, each year, tens of thousands of Gen Zers graduate college, launch careers, earn a full-time salary, rent apartments, apply for credit cards, purchase products and graduate to adulthood. That milestone transition from college to career is the inspiration for this book, *Gen Z Graduates To Adulthood*.

Unlike my first two Gen Z books, this book focuses less on what Gen Z is doing and more on what they are looking for in the future from marketers and employers. Aside from the inspiration that the oldest Gen Zers are now adults, another source of inspiration came from a question that was asked of me during one of the Gen Z keynote speeches that I delivered in 2021. One of the attendees asked, "Where does Gen Z want to be in 10 years?" I could not answer the question as it was one of the few questions that I had never been asked about Gen Z. The fact that I could not answer that one question was a challenge that I could not resist. At that moment, I decided that I would author my third Gen Z book with an exclusive focus on the oldest members of Gen Z, those who had graduated college in the past few years or who were expected to graduate as members of the class of 2022.

Unlike my two previous Gen Z books, I relied less on secondary research for this book and more on primary research. Aside from asking the oldest members of Gen Z questions I always ask regarding their preferred content channels, favorites brands and passions and interests, I asked them four questions.

What advice do you have for marketers attempting to covert you into a customer?

What advice do you have for potential future employers attempting to recruit and retain you and other Gen Zers?

What societal issue is important to you and why?

What are your aspirations and dreams over the next 10 years?

Aside from my commentary, this book features the words of more than 60 of the oldest members of Generation Z in response to those four questions. If you are a brand marketer, this book will provide insights directly from the minds and mouths of Gen Z that will inspire effective marketing and engagement through 2030. If you are an employer or work in human resources, this book will deliver the insights you need to successfully recruit and retain Gen Z employees. If you are a member of any organization where Gen Z is critical to your future success such as a university alumni association or a non-profit charity attempting to engage the next generation of volunteers and donors, *Gen Z Graduates To Adulthood* is the essential guide to understanding and effectively engaging the next most important consumer segment, Generation Z.

Part 1

Gen Z Glossary

Gen Z Glossary

Addy: Address

Adulting: Having to take on adult responsibilities

Banger: A great party

Bangin: Usually said as "That's Bangin" or "Banging," meaning super good

Basic: A person who gives into trends and has no originality

Bet: Wholeheartedly agreeing to something; meaning "yes" or "okay" or when someone challenges you, it's another way of saying, "we'll see about that," or "try me"

Bible: I swear, or I promise

Bit: Discussing your personal bitmoji or someone else's bitmoji

Bop: A really good song

Bot: Dumb

Boujee/Bougie: Someone who has lavish, expensive, extravagant tastes

Bread: Money

Bruh: Gender-neutral term used for a friend

Bussin: Used to describe something as great such as food or fashion.

Butter: Smooth

Cancel/Canceled: to stop supporting a celebrity or company, usually through boycotting their work or content and/or not buying their products

Can't Even: Unable to comprehend

Cap/Capping: To lie. "This person is capping."

Catch These Hands: To fight

Cheugy: Lifestyle trends associated with early 2010s, the opposite of trendy

Chill: Cool

Clout: Defines your level of coolness

Clowning: Being self-deprecating, being made a fool of

Crib: House

Cringy: Something that make somebody cringe

Cuffing: Getting into a relationship

Ded: Finding something extremely hilarious

Deep In The Cut: Far away

Dope: Very cool

Drag: Roasting someone via clever insults

Draking: Feeling emotional, sad

Drip: Cool clothes, sense of style, someone wearing expensive items

Drop A Pin: Sharing your current location with someone via text

Extra: Someone who is considered high maintenance, has a strong personality, tries too hard

Extreme Ghosting: Aside from not responding to text messages, a person blocks someone else from accessing their social media and blocks their incoming phone calls

Fact/Facts: Agreeing with a statement, truth

Fam: Close friends or someone's inner circle of friends

Fein: Craving something

Finna: Something's gonna happen

Finesse/Finessed: Doing something in a slick way, with ease, tricky someone into giving you something

Finsta: A fake Instagram account

Fire: Anything that looks good, sounds good, is good or really cool

Fit: Simply referring to an outfit, complimenting someone's outfit

Flame: To roast or make fun of another person

Flex: To show off your expensive possessions

Fire: Very good

FR: For real

From The Jump: From the beginning

Gas: You thought

Gassing You Up: Schmoozing someone

Go Ahead: Go for it, offering support to a friend

Go Off/Pop Off: To encourage or support a particular behavior like tell their story

Goals: Something to aspire to

GOAT: Greatest of all-time

Ghosted/Ghosting: One person intentionally stops responding to another person's text

Glo Up/Glow Up/Glowing Up: Someone who has gone through an incredible transformation, more mature. Confident, attractive

Guap: A significant amount of money

Gucci: Doing well

Handle: Instagram or Twitter username, "What's your IG handle?"

Highkey: Something that is so obvious to everyone and does not require explanation

Hits Different: Emphasizing how good something is or that stands out from the rest

HMU: Hit me up, inviting someone to contact you

Hype: Really excited

Hypebeast: Someone who wears the most popular clothes and follows the trends

Hype Up: To give a compliment/overly compliment
Ice: Cool jewelry

Iconic: Something that is memorable, a compliment for highly original and influential people

Ight: Alright

Imma: I'm going to

I'm Crying: Hysterically laughing

I'm Dead: A reaction to something very funny

I'm Done: You have nothing else to say or comment

I'm Down: An affirmation, "I'm down for that concert."

In My Bag: Feeling emotional

Instafamous: Getting an exceedingly high number of likes on Instagram without having celebrity status

Instagramable: An image or video that is worth putting on your Instagram channel

It's A Dub: Someone who you don't believe is worth your time

L: A losing situation

Left On Read: Somebody who is not replying to your text message

Let's Get This Bread: A motivational phrase to make money or go after money

Live Your Best Life: Enjoying life to the fullest

Living Rent Free: When you can't stop thinking of something

Lit: Something or someone that you think is awesome, cool, amazing

LMR: Asking someone to go to Instagram and like the recent image you posted

Lowkey: Something that is intended to be secret or not talked about

Mad: Excessive amounts of something

Main Character: Someone who draws others in, someone who is well liked

Me: Another way of saying, "Me too"

Mid: Average

Mood: Agreeing with someone's actions, feelings or plan

Move: It's what's going on or what's happening (see The Wave)

No Cap: No lie, for real. "No cap, I got a 100 on my exam"

Nowstalgia: Reliving early 2000s fashion trends

NP: No problem

Nugget: Anything that is adorable

OD: You are doing too much

OK Boomer: Meant as an insult to a member of an older generation after they make some sort of ignorant out-of-touch comment

On Point: Perfect, well done

Peep: To check-out/to look at

Peep My Tweet: Asking someone to go to your Twitter account and favorite your tweet

Periodt: Add emphasis to make a point

Piping Hot Tea: Really big gossip

Pressed: Being mad or upset about something

Pull Up: Hang out

Quality: Complimenting someone on the quality of their social post

Quaking: Shocked in a positive way

Read: Pointing out a flaw or inconsistency with someone's personality or story

Respect: A response to someone who has done something that you think is impressive

Salty: Mad, jealous, angry, upset

Same: Same here

Scoop: Pick me up

Secure The Bag: Getting money or accomplishing goals

Send It/Full Send: To fully commit to something

Sending Me: Used to describe how funny something is

Shade: To be sketchy or sneaky

Sheesh: Hyping someone up for looking good or doing something good

Shook: To be completely rattled or surprised by something

Shoot Your Shot: Taking a chance and going after an opportunity that may appear to be beyond someone's capability like attempting to be hired for a certain internship or job

Shots Fired: When someone makes a comment/joke at another person

Simp: Pouring your heart out for someone or going above and beyond for your significant other

Sis: Greeting for a close friend

Slaps: Something that is really good. "That song slaps."

Sliding Into Someone's DM: Direct message someone via Instagram/Twitter you want to meet

SMH: Shaking My Head when disappointed or embarrassed

Snack: A term describing someone who you find attractive

Snap Strike: When you delete Snapchat from your phone but don't delete your account

Snatched: Perfect, well done, something that looks really good like clothes

Spill the Tea: Hot gossip or information to share

Squad: Group of friends

Stan/We Stan: Stalker and fan, support enthusiastically, obsessed with a celebrity

Streak: A consecutive streak on Snapchat in which two people snap each other daily

SUP: "What's Up?"

Sus: A sketchy person who shouldn't be trusted

TBH: To be honest

Tea: Gossip

Thinking Ahead: Societal concerns affecting Gen Z

Tryna: Wanting to do something

TFW: That Feeling When...

That Ain't It Chief: Used in response to when you receive bad news

The Wave: It's what's going on or what's happening (a big event or party)

Thirsty: Someone who is desperate for attention and trying too hard

Thread: On Twitter, a person tells a story through a series of tweets

Triggered: To get annoyed, upset or sad, offended by someone else's actions

Thriving: Living your best life

Throw Hands: To fight

To Ship (someone/something): When you see people who look good together, you "ship" their relationship

Trill: A person who is considered genuine or real

Uncomfy: Uncomfortable

Unsult: A backhanded compliment

V: A substitute for "very," putting more emphasis and intensity on something

Vibe: Good energy

Vibe Check: Describing someone's vibe – if you fail the vibe check, that is a bad thing. If you pass the vie check, that means your likeable, fun, chill

Vibin': Enjoying something together like listening to music

Weak: When something is so funny or amusing

WFA: Work From Anywhere

WFH: Work From Home

Wig: Describing something that blows you away

Wig Flew: Funnier than Wig Snatched

Wig Snatched: Reading (see Read) someone to the point of embarrassment

WOAT: Worst of all-time

Woke: Being aware of current events and issues

Word: OK

Wyling: That's crazy

Yeet: Exclamation of excitement or to forcefully remove or throw

Yikes: In response to something cringy or inappropriate

You're Capping: You're lying

Yuur: Hello, catching someone's attention

Part II

Meet The Oldest Members Of Gen Z & Their Favorite Brands, Content Channels & Interests

ANTONIA A.
Age In 2022: 26
Occupation: Pharmaceutical Sales Representative
Favorite Brands: Lululemon, Target, Starbucks, Rook Coffee, Alo Yoga, Nike, Kith, Dunkin'
Favorite Social Media/Content Channels: Instagram, Snapchat, TikTok
Passions/Interests/Hobbies: Sports, Health/Wellness, Traveling, Food

BRIAN A.
Age In 2022: 25
Occupation: Public Relations
Favorite Brands: Patagonia, Nike, Lululemon, Apple, J. Crew
Favorite Social Media/Content Channels: Twitter, Instagram, YouTube, New York Times, Washington Post, NJ.com, APP.com
Passions/Interests/Hobbies: Watching Sports, Fitness, Politics, News, Restaurants/Food, Experiences

ALEXIS B.
Age In 2022: 24
Occupation: Marketing Coordinator
Favorite Brands: Lululemon, Crunch Fitness, Kate Spade, Apple
Favorite Social Media/Content Channels: Instagram, Snapchat, Reddit, YouTube
Passions/Interests/Hobbies: Fitness, Cooking, Reading

DANIELLE B.
Age In 2022: 24
Occupation: Brand Marketing
Favorite Brands: Rare Beauty, Bumble, Djerf Avenue
Favorite Social Media/Content Channels: Instagram, TikTok, YouTube
Passions/Interests/Hobbies: Journaling, Painting, Traveling

LAYSTON B.
Age In 2022: 25
Occupation: Innovation Operations
Favorite Brands: Bombas, Fitbit, Prose, Imperfect Foods, EarthHero Marketplace
Favorite Social Media/Content Channels: YouTube, Instagram, Reddit, LinkedIn, Discord
Passions/Interests/Hobbies: Financial Literacy, Personal Finance, Assisting Young Job Seekers, Cooking, Pilates, Strength Training, Vision Boarding, Travel

SAM B.
Age In 2022: 24
Occupation: Public Relations
Favorite Brands: Chipotle, Aerie, Lululemon, Apple Target
Favorite Social Media/Content Channels: Instagram, Snapchat, LinkedIn, TikTok
Passions/Interests/Hobbies: Cooking, Baking, Travel, Skiing, Music

SEAN BO.
Age In 2022: 25
Occupation: Graduate Student/Public Relations
Favorite Brands: Starbucks, Chipotle, Audi
Favorite Social Media/Content Channels: Instagram, Snapchat, YouTube, Twitter
Passions/Interests/Hobbies: Automotive, Sports, Fitness

SEAN BU.
Age In 2022: 24
Occupation: Sales/Marketing
Favorite Brands: RCVA, Barstool Sports, Red Bull
Favorite Social Media/Content Channels: Twitter, YouTube, TikTok
Passions/Interests/Hobbies: Fishing, Cooking, Sports, History, Comedy

BRITTANY C.
Age In 2022: 26

Occupation: Account Coordinator - Public Relations

Favorite Brands: Marshalls/TJ Maxx, Netflix, Trader Joe's, Express

Favorite Social Media/Content Channels: TikTok, Twitter (where I primarily seek news), Snapchat, YouTube, LinkedIn

Passions/Interests/Hobbies: Travel, Working Out, Jogging, The Beach, Hiking, Astrology

CARL C.
Age In 2022: 24

Occupation: Content Creator/Social Media Marketer

State Currently Living: NJ

Favorite Brands: Spotify, Adidas, Amazon

Favorite Social Media/Content Channels: Twitter, Instagram, Bleacher Report, LinkedIn, TikTok, Snapchat

Passions/Interests/Hobbies: Sports, Weightlifting/Fitness, Sports Cards/Collectibles

GIANNA C.
Age In 2022: 25

Occupation: Television Account Manager

Favorite Brands: Disney, Bravo, Abercrombie, Ulta, American Express

Favorite Social Media/Content Channels: YouTube, Instagram, TikTok, Facebook, Twitter

Passions/Interests/Hobbies: Travel, Working Out, Finding Great Restaurants

JENNA C.
Age In 2022: 25
Occupation: Marketing; Digital Media and Content Specialist
Favorite Brands: Starbucks, Apple, Abercrombie & Fitch
Favorite Social Media/Content Channels: Twitter, Snapchat, Instagram
Passions/Interests/Hobbies: Music, Cooking, Reading

LARA C.
Age In 2022: 26
Occupation: Data Analyst
Favorite Brands: Bottega Veneta, Starbucks, Target
Favorite Social Media/Content Channels: Instagram, YouTube, TikTok
Passions/Interests/Hobbies: Soccer, Fashion, Cooking

LAUREN C.
Age In 2022: 24
Occupation: Political Consultant
Favorite Brands: Aritzia, Louis Vitton, Breville
Favorite Social Media/Content Channels: Instagram, Twitter, YouTube
Passions/Interests/Hobbies: Playing Piano, Music, Cooking, Advocating for Civil Rights, Sports, Photography

MARGARET C.
Age In 2022: 22
Occupation: Corporate Social Responsibility Fellow
Favorite Brands: Johnson & Johnson, JEEP, Apple
Favorite Social Media/Content Channels: LinkedIn, Facebook, Instagram
Passions/Interests/Hobbies: Reading, Skiing, Binge Watching Medical Dramas

ASHLEY D.
Age In 2022: 26
Occupation: Medical Editor
Favorite Brands: Bath & Body Works, Michael's, Target
Favorite Social Media/Content Channels: TikTok, Reddit, YouTube, Instagram, Twitter, Pinterest
Passions/Interests/Hobbies: Art, Travel, Musical Theatre, Cooking, Film/Cinema

JENNA D.
Age In 2022: 25
Occupation: Corporate Communications
Favorite Brands: Target, Marshalls, T.J. Maxx, Netflix
Favorite Social Media/Content Channels: YouTube, Instagram/Pinterest
Passions/Interests/Hobbies: Health/Wellness, Cooking, Walking

JENNIFER D.
Age In 2022: 24
Favorite Brands: Dunkin', Apple, Everlane
Favorite Social Media/Content Channels: TikTok, Instagram, LinkedIn
Passions/Interests/Hobbies: Sewing, Crafting, Baking, Binge Watching Netflix

JOELLE D.
Age In 2022: 23
Occupation: Public Relations
Favorite Brands: Spotify, Amazon, Apple
Favorite Social Media/Content Channels: Facebook, TikTok, Twitter, Instagram
Passions/Interests/Hobbies: Reading, Baking, Music

SUMMER D.
Age In 2022: 26
Occupation: Entrepreneur/Marketer
Favorite Brands: Target, Amazon, Starbucks, Cricut
Favorite Social Media/Content Channels: TikTok, Instagram, Twitter
Passions/Interests/Hobbies: Creating, Cricut, Pop Culture, Seeking New Adventures
(kid friendly, walking trails, etc.)

TROY D.
Age In 2022: 23
Occupation: Account Management/Sales
Favorite Brands: Target, Taco Bell, Jersey Mike's Vans, Ray-Ban
Favorite Social Media/Content Channels: TikTok, Instagram, Twitter
Passions/Interests/Hobbies: Sports, Cars, Video Games, New Music

CRISTINA F.
Age In 2022: 24
Occupation: Creative Coordinator
Favorite Brands: Glossier, Charlotte Tilbury, Baggu, Wendy's, Zara
Favorite Social Media/Content Channels: Instagram, Pinterest, Twitter
Passions/Interests/Hobbies: Music, Songwriting, Roller Skating, Crocheting, Yoga

GABRIELLE F.
Age In 2022: 23
Occupation: Communications
Favorite Brands: Wawa, Lululemon, Jersey Mike's, Spotify
Favorite Social Media/Content Channels: TikTok, Twitter, Instagram
Passions/Interests/Hobbies: Content Creation, Fitness, Reading

OLIVIA F.
Age In 2022: 23
Occupation: Public Relations
Favorite Brands: Target, Sephora, Aerie
Favorite Social Media/Content Channels: Instagram, TikTok, Snapchat, Twitter, Pinterest
Passions/Interests/Hobbies: Make Up, Skin Care, Reading, Music

ADAM G.
Age In 2022: 24
Occupation: Assistant Paid Media Manager
Favorite Brands: Hoonigan, Donut Media, Lululemon, &Pizza, Porsche, Honda, Nissan, Mercedes, BMW, YouTube, RA Guide, Dice.FM, SoundCloud
Favorite Social Media/Content Channels: Instagram, Snapchat, Facebook, YouTube, TikTok
Passions/Interests/Hobbies: Golf, Skiing, Weightlifting, Healthy Eating, Paleo Diet, Music, Cars, Hiking

KATIE G.
Age in 2022: 26
Occupation: Public Relations
Favorite Brands: Abercrombie, Sephora, Truff
Favorite Social Media/Content Channels: TikTok, Twitter, Pinterest
Passions/Interests/Hobbies: Live Music, Fitness, Travel

PARIS G.
Age in 2022: 24
Occupation: Social Media/Content Creation
Favorite Brands: Nike, HBO, Sony, Apple, Calvin Klein, BMW
Favorite Social Media/Content Channels: Instagram, Snapchat, Discord, YouTube
Passions/Interests/Hobbies: Sports, Gaming, Fashion, History, Automobiles, Podcasting, Art, Music

PAT G.
Age In 2022: 22
Occupation: Assistant Communications Director
Favorite Brands: Lululemon, Patagonia, Rook Coffee, Chipotle, Vineyard Vines
Favorite Social Media/Content Channels: TikTok, LinkedIn, Twitter, Reddit, HBO Max, Hulu
Passions/Interests/Hobbies: Politics, Restaurants, Music, Fishing

ALESSANDRA I.
Age In 2022: 22
Occupation: Marketing/Public Relations/Events
Favorite Brands: Herschel, Wolven, Nike
Favorite Social Media/Content Channels: Instagram, YouTube, TikTok
Passions/Interests/Hobbies: Dance, Music, Food, Travel

RYAN J.
Age In 2022: 22
Occupation: Account Manager, Food Sciences
Favorite Brands: Taco Bell, Buffalo Wild Wings, Chipotle, Sperry, American Eagle, SpaceX, NASA, BMW
Favorite Social Media/Content Channels: Snapchat, Instagram, TikTok, YouTube, LinkedIn
Passions/Interests/Hobbies: Food Industry, Space, Movies, Classic Rock

GILLIAN K.
Age In 2022: 22
Occupation: Digital Marketing
Favorite Brands: Target, Dunkin', Starbucks, H&M
Favorite Social Media/Content Channels: TikTok, Instagram, Pinterest
Passions/Interests/Hobbies: Outdoor Sports, Singing, Reading, Gardening

HANNAH K.
Age In 2022: 22
Occupation: Public Relations
Favorite Brands: Apple, Amazon, Dunkin'
Favorite Social Media/Content Channels: TikTok, YouTube, Instagram
Passions/Interests/Hobbies: Cooking, Traveling, Writing Poems

KAYLA L.
Age In 2022: 26
Occupation: Graduate Student
Favorite Brands: Netflix, Abercrombie, Ulta
Favorite Social Media/Content Channels: Instagram, TikTok, YouTube
Passions/Interests/Hobbies: Music, Travel, Fitness

KYMANI L.
Age In 2022: 24
Occupation: Content Creator
Favorite Brands: Nike, Adidas, Apple, Marvel, Foot Locker, Coca-Cola
Favorite Social Media/Content Channels: Instagram, Twitter, TikTok
Passions/Interests/Hobbies: Music, Movies, Television, Basketball

MICAH L.
Age In 2022: 26
Occupation: Account Manager/Marketing Project Management
Favorite Brands: Staple Pigeon, Crocs, New Balance
Favorite Social Media/Content Channels: TikTok, Snapchat, Instagram, LinkedIn, Venmo
Passions/Interests/Hobbies: Beatboxing, Soccer, Entomology

RACHEL L.
Age In 2022: 22
Occupation: Marketing/Public Relations
Favorite Brands: Trader Joe's, Ben & Jerry's, American Eagle
Favorite Social Media/Content Channels: TikTok, Instagram, Snapchat, Tumblr, Reddit, Twitter
Passions/Interests/Hobbies: Food Blogging, Adult Sports Leagues, Reading

HANALEE M.
Age In 2022: 25
Occupation: Product Development Assistant
Favorite Brands: I don't really have brands that I am super loyal to! I like to mix things up with my wardrobe, I thrift and love trying new boutiques. Some brands I can say I have favored are The Cheesecake Factory, New Balance, Converse, Goodwill
Favorite Social Media/Content Channels: Instagram, Snapchat, Pinterest
Passions/Interests/Hobbies: Travel, Health, Fashion

MATILDA M.
Age In 2022: 24
Occupation: Public Relations/Marketing
Favorite Brands: Lululemon, Target, Apple
Favorite Social Media/Content Channels: TikTok, Instagram, Snapchat, Facebook, Pinterest, Reddit
Passions/Interests/Hobbies: Running, Traveling To New Countries And Exploring Cultures

SARAH M.
Age In 2022: 25
Occupation: Public Relations
Favorite Brands: Ben & Jerry's, Patagonia, Gymshark
Favorite Social Media/Content Channels: Twitter, Instagram, TikTok
Passions/Interests/Hobbies: Running, Reading, Baking

JULIANNA N.
Age In 2022: 25
Occupation: Public Relations
Favorite Brands: Ulta, Target, Abercrombie, Uber, Netflix, Chick-fil-A
Favorite Social Media/Content Channels: TikTok, Instagram, Snapchat, Pinterest
Passions/Interests/Hobbies: Live Music, Sports, Travel

FRANKIE P.
Age In 2022: 24
Occupation: Marketing
Favorite Brands: Lululemon, Ben & Jerry's Patagonia
Favorite Social Media/Content Channels: TikTok, Instagram, Reddit, LinkedIn
Passions/Interests/Hobbies: Sports (Skiing, Tennis, Field Hockey), Fitness, Travel

MICHAEL P.
Age In 2022: 23
Occupation: Strategy Consulting with Marketing specialization
Favorite Brands: Patagonia, Dunkin', Nike
Favorite Social Media/Content Channels: Instagram, Snapchat, YouTube
Passions/Interests/Hobbies: Fitness, Psychology, Sports

SARAH P.
Age In 2022: 24
Occupation: Freelancer (copywriter, actor, dance educator, film production person)
Favorite Brands: Burju, Barbie, Apple, EDWINS, Duolingo, Slack, Marshall's
Favorite Social Media/Content Channels: TikTok, Facebook, LinkedIn, Instagram, Pangea.app, Spotify
Passions/Interests/Hobbies: Acting, Eating, Dancing

ALYSSA R.
Age In 2022: 24
Occupation: Experiential Marketing
Favorite Brands: Netflix, HBO Max, Nike
Favorite Social Media/Content Channels: Instagram, YouTube, Facebook, Snapchat, NPR, CNN
Passions/Interests/Hobbies: Sports, Travel, Entertainment (TV/Film)

FLOR R.
Age In 2022: 24
Occupation: Event Producer
Favorite Brands: Nike, Ben & Jerry's, Spotify
Favorite Social Media/Content Channels: YouTube, Reddit, LinkedIn, Pinterest, Twitter, TikTok
(not good for me, but I'm always on it)
Passions/Interests/Hobbies: Music, Traveling, Networking, Fitness

KYLIE R.
Age In 2022: 25
Occupation: Teacher
Favorite Brands: Amazon, Apple, Disney
Favorite Social Media/Content Channels: Twitter, TikTok, The Wall Street Journal (digital)
Passions/Interests/Hobbies: Reading, Cooking, Gardening

ROYA R.
Age In 2022: 23
Occupation: Public Relations
Favorite Brands: Apple, Target, Trader Joe's, Starbucks, BMW, Aerie, Abercrombie & Fitch, UGG, Lush Cosmetics, The North Face, Hulu, Netflix, Ray-Ban
Favorite Social Media/Content Channels: Instagram, Snapchat, Twitter, TikTok, YouTube
Passions/Interests/Hobbies: Sports, Travel, Cooking

SHELBY R.
Age In 2022: 26
Occupation: Public Relations
Favorite Brands: Sephora, CeraVe, Abercrombie, Patagonia
Favorite Social Media/Content Channels: TikTok, Twitter, Instagram, LinkedIn
Passions/Interests/Hobbies: Food/Cooking, Travel, Creative Writing

SYDNEY R.
Age In 2022: 22
Occupation: Public Relations
Favorite Brands: Zara, Alo Yoga, PJ Salvage
Favorite Social Media/Content Channels: Instagram, Snapchat, TikTok
Passions/Interests/Hobbies: Exercise, Making A Difference In Other's Lives, Reading, Cooking/Baking

GENO S.
Age In 2022: 25
Occupation: Community Manager
Favorite Brands: Aldi
Favorite Social Media/Content Channels: Instagram, LinkedIn, Twitter
Passions/Interests/Hobbies: Fitness, Friends, Family"

HAILLEY S.
Age In 2022: 25
Occupation: Public Relations
Favorite Brands: Urban Outfitters, Chipotle, Doc Martens, Vans, Trader Joe's, Spotify
Favorite Social Media/Content Channels: TikTok, Twitter, YouTube, Instagram, Snapchat
Passions/Interests/Hobbies: Music, Food, Ceramics (art), Feminism (social justice)

ISAIAH S.
Age In 2022: 23
Occupation: Customer Support Specialist
Favorite Brands: Nike, Nintendo, Pokemon
Favorite Social Media/Content Channels: Twitter, Instagram, Reddit
Passions/Interests/Hobbies: Video Games, Reading Novels/Comic Books, Exercise, Watching Jeopardy

REBEKAH S.
Age In 2022: 23
Occupation: Journalist
Favorite Brands: Nintendo, Dunkin', Ulta, Starbucks, Bath & Body Works
Favorite Social Media/Content Channels: YouTube, Twitter, Instagram, Reddit
Passions/Interests/Hobbies: Writing, Food, Music, Gaming

RYAN S.
Age In 2022: 24
Occupation: Public Relations
Favorite Brands: Nike, Ben & Jerry's, Patagonia
Favorite Social Media/Content Channels: TikTok, Twitter, LinkedIn, Barstool Sports, Bleacher Report
Passions/Interests/Hobbies: Running, Watching Sports, Networking, Mentoring

SAMANTHA S.
Age In 2022: 25
Occupation: High School Paraprofessional for Special Education Program
Favorite Brands: Target, Playa Bowls, Coors Light, TJ Maxx, Wawa
Favorite Social Media/Content Channels: Instagram, Snapchat, TikTok, Pinterest, YouTube
Passions/Interests/Hobbies: Philadelphia Sports, Shopping, Food

ISABEAU T.
Age In 2022: 25
Occupation: Public Relations
Favorite Brands: Kids of Immigrants, Telfar, Airbnb
Favorite Social Media/Content Channels: Instagram, TikTok, Twitter, Pinterest, Reddit
Passions/Interests/Hobbies: Travel, Music, Food

RACHEL U.
Age In 2022: 24
Occupation: Graduate Student
Favorite Brands: Target, Athleta, Adidas
Favorite Social Media/Content Channels: Snapchat, Instagram, TikTok, NBC News
Passions/Interests/Hobbies: Working Out, Hanging Out With Friends/Family, Going To The Beach, Baking

DAVID W.
Age In 2022: 22
Occupation: Public Relations Intern
Favorite Brands: Nike, Starbucks, Apple
Favorite Social Media/Content Channels: Twitter, Snapchat, YouTube
Passions/Interests/Hobbies: Sports, Music, Mental Health Awareness

NICOLE W.
Age In 2022: 24
Occupation: Social Media & Marketing
Favorite Brands: Apple, Amazon, Spotify
Favorite Social Media/Content Channels: TikTok, Instagram, Snapchat, TEDx, Bleacher Report
Passions/Interests/Hobbies: Fitness, Reading, Travel, Music, Sports

OLIVER W.
Age In 2022: 24
Occupation: Marketing
Favorite Brands: Netflix, Ben & Jerry's, Apple, Lululemon
Favorite Social Media/Content Channels: Now This News, Now This Earth, Complex, Red Bull Unilever, Instagram, TikTok, Snapchat
Passions/Interests/Hobbies: Golf, Travel, Soccer

NICHOLAS Y.
Age In 2022: 25
Occupation: Public Relations
Favorite Brands: Apple, Adidas, Jeep, DraftKings, Sony, Marvel, Taco Bell, Amazon
Favorite Social Media/Content Channels:
New Rockstars on YouTube, Broadcast Boys on TikTok, Twitter
Passions/Interests/Hobbies: Movies, TV Shows, Podcasts, Sports, Sports Betting, Hiking, Eating, Cooking

Part III

Advice for Marketers

Advice for Marketers

Accicording to a November 17, 2021 story in Bloomberg, Gen Z has $360 billion in spending power. The article credits that number to the fact that each year, more Gen Zers are graduating college and working full-time jobs and earning income from side businesses. It's one of the reasons why I authored this book. It's also a primary reason why Gen Z is becoming a priority for brand marketers.

When I present my Gen Z keynote speech to companies and conferences, I introduce the concept of a paradigm shift from the marketing and advertising that consumer brands have utilized for many years to attract consumers including millennials, Gen X and boomers, to effectively engaging Generation Z, a segment that does not consume traditional media such as television and does not respond to traditional

Pollard, A. (2021, November 17). *Gen Z Has $360 Billion To Spend, Trick Is Getting Them To Spend*. Bloomberg. Retrieved from https://www.bloomberg.com/news/articles/2021-11-17/gen-z-has-360-billion-to-spend-trick-is-getting-them-to-buy#:~:text=The%20cohort%20has%20%24360%20billion,advisory%20firm%20Gen%20Z%20Planet.

marketing. Not only is Gen Z consuming content primarily on channels that did not exist 20 years ago including YouTube, Instagram, TikTok and Snapchat, but they are looking to be engaged before they will even consider becoming a customer and potentially an advocate for a brand.

In the previous section of this book, I introduced more than 60 of the oldest members of Gen Z and their favorite brands and content channels. Those insights provide valuable clues for marketers in 2022 and beyond.

First, Gen Z's preferred content channels are unprecedented when compared to previous generations. Very few of the Gen Zers who were surveyed mentioned cable or network television as a favorite content channel. For a marketer, that should be an immediate lightbulb moment. If Gen Z is becoming a priority or the priority for your brand, you need to throw away your media buying playbook that you utilized to market to millennials. Gen Zers are not millennials and they do not consume media the way millennials did when they may have been the primary focus for many brand marketers.

Second, review the brands that Gen Zers claim are their favorites. You will see brands such as Target, Patagonia, Spotify and others repeatedly referenced. As a marketer, you can learn why these brands are loved by Gen Z. Target is the first consumer brand that I am aware of that launched a Gen Z incubator in 2018 to connect and collaborate with Gen Z. They have consistently collaborated with Gen Zers nationwide over the past five years and it has informed and inspired their marketing. Patagonia's mission to, "save our home planet" is the purpose-led approach that engages Gen Z, the purpose generation. Spotify not only delivers value to a generation in which many members are just starting their careers, but Spotify's personalization and customization of playlists is the type of offering that engages this cohort and what they are looking for in other products and services they purchase.

In my ongoing survey of Gen Zers nationwide in the United States, consistently, 80 percent agree that access, events and experiences are the most effective way to engage this cohort. Those experiences are not only engaging, but they lead to the most powerful form of marketing, a Gen Z consumer producing and distributing content on their social media channels as a result of a brand offering them a unique experience. This is commonly referred to as an Instagramable experience. I believe it is one of the reasons why *The Wall Street Journal* featured a story on January 27, 2022, titled, "NBA Teams Add Chief Experience Officers to Their C-Suite." Aside from sports leagues, the article highlights that companies such as Best Buy and Volkswagen have appointed executives as chief experience officers recently. One executive was quoted saying, "experience is the currency of business." Gen Z agrees.

Alcantara, A.-M. (2022, January 27). *NBA Teams Add Chief Experience Officers To Their C-Suites*. The Wall Street Journal. Retrieved from https://www.wsj.com/articles/nba-teams-add-chief-experience-officers-to-their-c-suites-11643322024

Prior to the pandemic, the Taco Bell Hotel was an example of an experience that the brand offered that engaged Gen Z whether physically in-person or via the content that Taco Bell shared on their owned media channels. Target's incubator is an example of a unique experience that engages Gen Zers nationwide as is the Converse All-Stars program and the National Hockey League's Power Players Gen Z advisory board. On a lighter side, campaigns such as Bud Light Seltzer's search for a Chief Meme Officer, Doritos' search via TikTok for a 'flavor confirmer' and McCormick's search for a Director of Taco Relations, are all examples of marketing campaigns that offer access and experiences that engage Gen Z.

Locally or nationally, any company or brand has the ability to offer unique access, events and experiences. As a first step, I invite marketers to simply audit every asset they have under their roof that could be converted into an experience. To bring this concept to life, I use the example of a Zamboni which resurfaces the ice between periods of a hockey game. Now, imagine you are handling marketing for a hockey team in the National Hockey League, AHL or ECHL. Take that one asset of the Zamboni machine which was simply considered functional and now offer access to Gen Zers to sit in the passenger seat between periods of a game. By the time the seven-minute ice resurfacing is completed, the Gen Zer in the passenger seat who was provided the unique access, event and experience, will have produced and distributed content promoting the hockey team's brand across

TikTok, Snapchat, Instagram and other content channels engaging their Gen Z friends and followers, those who they influence the most more than any celebrity or social media influencer.

Consistently, when I survey Gen Zers nationwide in the United States, more than one third claim that the biggest influencers in their lives are their Gen Z friends who they follow on social media. Gen Z friends have greater influence than celebrities such as athletes and actors as well as individuals who are famous for producing and distributing content on channels such as TikTok and Instagram. For marketers, that is a critical insight. It's one reason why I recommend brands and organizations develop and mobilize a team of Gen Z ambassadors similar to what Major League Baseball did in 2021 when they introduced their inaugural Creator Class comprised of 11 content creators. While these content creators may not be household names, they exude influence.

A think tank or incubator program like those mentioned previously from Target, Converse and the National Hockey League also serve as great spheres of influence that could evolve into Gen Z ambassador programs. When Target launched their Gen Z incubator in 2018, their executive vice president and chief marketing officer, Rick Gomez, stated what every brand marketer should be doing in 2022 and beyond if they want to effectively engage Gen Z. "To truly engage our next generation of guests, it's not enough to create great brands. We need to cultivate communities and have real conversations. So, we're using our expertise and brand power to connect with our young guests, amplify their voices and support their great ideas for the future."

In the spirit of Rick's words and Target's innovative approach to, "connect with our young guests, amplify their voices and support their great ideas for the future," on the following pages are insightful ideas and advice from the voices of more than 60 of the oldest Gen Zers for brand marketers who want to effectively engage Gen Z.

"I think the best way for businesses to market is through deals/promos on Instagram at least for me. I tend to see a post from one of my favorite brands on their personal Instagram page about a new launch or sale and I am engaged, consume and often purchase. I definitely dislike sponsored ads. Most Gen Zers skip sponsored ads and don't pay attention."

—Antonia A.

"Be relatable; be conscious of current issues, movements, and trends; treat employees the way you describe in your job postings. Consumers — specifically Gen Z — are willing to spend on quality products and services from quality companies."

—Brian A

"Know what consumers want before they do."

—Alexis B.

"Marketing in a creative way with a clear and defined purpose is so important in today's world. With trends changing every day and activism being at the forefront of our media consumption, brands need to be agile and willing to meet the needs of the consumer while still catering to relevant societal injustices. Tackling this is complex and should amplify the voices of those widely affected. This creates space for genuine and authentic content which consumers really connect with."

—Danielle B.

DID YOU KNOW?

32% of Gen Zers claim Instagram is their favorite social media channel followed by TikTok (28%), but Snapchat leads the way for Gen Zers who are still in high school

Source: Mark Beal Survey of Generation Z in the United States, September 2021

"Be genuine in their messaging and what they stand for. We're a much more socially, environmentally, and brand conscious generation. Cash grabs, greenwashing, and performative acts are not going to build brand loyalty. I'm willing to invest more money in a company that produces high-quality products and supports environmentalism or another societal issue. Transparency and action to improve when there is an issue speaks wonders for a company and helps in that long-term goal."

—Layston B.

"When I'm looking to purchase something, I want the product to be reliable and the customer service to be exceptional and convenient. If I have to jump through hoops or pay extra to return my product if I'm not satisfied, I'm hesitant to purchase that product. Putting the customer first in terms of product and service will win my loyalty."

—Sam B.

DID YOU KNOW?

When it comes to all content platforms, Gen Z's "Big Three" are TikTok (23%), Instagram (21%) and YouTube (20%).

Source: Mark Beal Survey of Generation Z in the United States, September 2021

"Provide customers with an experience they cannot get elsewhere. Consider bringing settings and elements from television, content and advertising and converting those into real-life experiences that Gen Z can participate in and share on their social media channels."

—Sean Bo.

"My advice to marketers looking to convert my generation into customers over the next decade is to try and pertain to us as people, and not consumers. What I mean by that is, market to our interests, our sense of humor, partner with entertainers/influencers, and other things of that nature, rather than just us as consumers. My generation aligns our consumer habits between our personalities and respective companies, people, and missions."

—Sean Bu.

"Have a meaningful message, something that is going to make me feel connected to your brand. I've found myself seeking out brands that also seek to empower or look to leave the world better than they found it (Patagonia, Youth to the People, Rare Beauty, etc.). I also like when brands partner with influencers/celebs that aren't just in it for the money, but clearly care about what they promote (Lauren Lane comes to mind immediately)."

—Brittany C.

"Market towards a memory. One of my favorite marketing techniques by companies like Spotify and Snapchat is that their campaigns touch on what you did in the past year. For example, Spotify wrapped goes over your minutes, top artists and more from the past year. This is a main factor in why I stick with them over other streaming services."

—Carl C.

DID YOU KNOW?

YouTube (14%) leads the way as Gen Z's top destination for news and information followed by Twitter (11%) and Instagram (10%).

Source: Mark Beal Survey of Generation Z in the United States, September 2021

"My advice to markers is to stop trying so hard and convert customers with ease. This can be done by using strategic decisions that will benefit the product or brand they are trying to promote. One powerful way to convert viewers into customers is by the use of content integrations. When a product fits seamlessly within a certain program this could turn the eyeballs that watch a certain show or movie into customers. It is important to note that a seamless integration is key here, forcing a product into a program that can be obviously spotted could leave a sour taste in the viewer's mind. The last thing marketers want is Gen Z poking fun at their brand and how they promote it. The viewers have the power now and forever."

—Gianna C.

"When it comes to purchasing items through the internet, I am constantly impressed with the ad work I see through social media algorithms. For instance, innovative strategies that are eye catching include 'themes' or collaborations of brands x nostalgic design. What comes to mind, is the ColourPop makeup brand that dropped a Lizzie McGuire line. This captured the interest of those who grew up watching the Disney show and have turned into makeup lovers."

—Jenna C.

"Make the product or service so embedded in society and daily life that I literally can't function without it such as Uber."

—Lara C.

"It is crucial for marketers to understand the various modes of media that Gen Zers consume on a daily basis as well as to have a reliable network of people to utilize the trends and jargon that tends to be used exclusively by Gen Zers."

—Lauren C.

"I would push marketers to continue to use TikTok influencers to market products to this generation. There have been a few times where influencers have reviewed a product that I really liked and they linked it to Amazon or another vendor and I went and checked it out on that external site. I have not always purchased the products, but it got my attention enough to bring me to the other site or to put the product in my Amazon cart."

—Margaret C.

"In order to reach Gen Z as an audience, you have to have a genuine brand and voice. I am unlikely to purchase a product that's shown in a banner ad on a website or as a sponsored post on social media. What makes the biggest difference, to me, is casual use of a product by friends or influencers. Posts or videos that are only made with "#ad" under them will also not convince me to be a customer; if anything, it makes me not want to be one. So, the best way to convert me into a customer is to be a brand with ethics and a genuine way of advertising instead of forced exposure."

—Ashley D.

"If you want to market to me, people like me must be represented in your materials."

—Jenna D.

"As an individual who is looking to minimize waste by purchasing goods of higher quality, I often look to the marketing to understand how the product is made and where the materials are sourced. Is the brand I am purchasing from using better materials with more strength and longevity? Does the company have a tighter manufacturing tolerance, or a great product warranty? Companies that are transparent about where they source their materials and that are willing to stand behind their products by offering strong warranties or the ability to send product back to be fixed (i.e., Patagonia's Return, Repair, and Exchanges policy) are those that stand out the most to me."

—Jennifer D.

DID YOU KNOW?

YouTube is Gen Z's favorite destination for video content, and they spend significant time there.
30%: View YouTube 3-9 Times A Day
27%: View YouTube 1- 2 Times A Day
26%: View YouTube 10+ Times A Day

Source: Mark Beal Survey of Generation Z in the United States, September 2021

"My favorite campaigns always make me laugh, so that's always a good tactic to use, especially for young people on social media."

—Joelle D.

"Gen Z is all about authenticity. No one likes a 'try hard.' We want everything to be genuine and natural, and we are more inclined to relate. The new Sex In The City show tries to be so politically correct with gender and talk about COVID that it takes away from the show, in a way that is not natural."

—Summer D.

"Be creative (and funny) in your marketing efforts. The brands that have captured the attention of Gen Z the best such as Duolingo on TikTok or Wendy's on Twitter use a comedic approach that resonates with our generation. Traditional ad placement and campaigns spark very little interest to most of Gen Z, but when the official Twitter page for Wendy›s makes fun of random people for choosing to go to Burger King, we tend to have a much more memorable impression."

—Troy D.

"Be authentic in your advertising and social media content."

—Cristina F.

"I encourage marketers to not try and fit in with what is popular but to stand out with new ideas in order to attract customers. Gen Z is a generation that takes past movements and turns them into new trends and innovative ideas. The world is going to keep changing so don't try to fit in, just make sure you keep up."

—Gabrielle F.

"Brands should be inclusive of all people, regardless of size, socioeconomic status, and race."

—Olivia F.

"Really try to put yourself in the shoes of your target audience, be relatable, but more importantly, be sympathetic. Feel for what your customers are going through and establish relationships upon this basis of not understanding but trying to understand and be there for them with the solution you provide. This more personal and intimate approach comes off way less salesy and would make me more intrigued/inclined to learn more about whatever marketing initiative I'm being delivered."

—Adam G.

"My generation is in the unique position of having known both a world without the internet and smartphones in our first few years of our lives but then also growing up as these technologies were dawning, around the time we were in late elementary school – so we learned to use them as the creators/CEOs of these tools were bettering their capabilities. Our brains are wired this way, and now they are fully integrated into our lives. I personally am so bombarded by advertisements on every platform – even while doing my job – that a return to authenticity and genuine customer service has become paramount for me. If a brand is willing to invest in customer service and can provide an easy path from marketing a product to me all the way through purchase, I'm much more likely to become a brand loyalist. I want to buy from brands that are inclusive – whether that be clothing brands who serve a range of body types or makeup brands that ensure a massive range of skin tones – I want to know that the brand I chose to spend my money on is thinking about ALL buyers."

—Katie G.

"In order for marketers to grasp my interest and convince me to invest into their company, they need to first gain my trust. Once gained, the product needs to be beneficial in some way or another as far as the value it brings into my immediate life."

—Paris G.

"Gen Z definitely buys into brands more than previous generations. We are happy paying a little more for something if we are a fan of the brand. It is why Target is widely popular despite Walmart offering may of the same products for cheaper. Doing things such as direct engagement with consumers on social media, advocating for social causes, and utilizing Gen Z's favorite influencers for promotion are valuable investments in cultivating a brand following."

—Pat G.

"I like a brand that is genuine and does not really care to beat its competitors or endlessly expand. If a brand is themself and is passionate about what they do, they should attract the right customers and continue to succeed for who they are. For example, I used to enjoy Panera food/ drinks when I was a young girl, but as they have grown in popularity and knew they could make a profit expanding, I believe the quality of their products has decreased. I don't know if this is all in my head, but it is what I believe."

—Alessandra I.

"We are at a point now where sustainability, environmental consciousness, and corporate social responsibility are some of the most important topics we face in the world today and going forward for years to come. My advice to marketers would be to reflect how they are positively acting upon these topics through their company values which are backed by credible actions in their messages and relations to consumers."

—Ryan J.

"The younger generations care more about the 'who' of a company than flashy marketing techniques. I actively search for brands that use recycled materials, are kind to animals, and have humanitarian relief programs in their business model. I also look for any news on how a company is treating their employees or where they stand politically. While it can be a hassle, I do this research and firmly stay away from brands that do not align with my values because I recognize the power that large corporations have in this world."

—Gillian K.

"Gen Z is a generation that wants to be understood. We connect better with marketers that choose to share a story rather than sell one and ones that understand the obstacles that we have faced growing up in the digital age."

—Hannah K.

"Emotional and moral conditions have a greater chance of changing a person's attitudes or behaviors."

—Kayla L.

"Gen Z appreciates marketing campaigns that are genuine in their approach: don't try to bait and switch us or sell to us in a way that makes us doubt the authenticity of a brand and their messaging."

Kymani L.

"Give your product personality."

Micah L.

DID YOU KNOW?

80% of Gen Zers agree that unique experiences, events and access are the most effective way for marketers to engage them.

Source: Mark Beal Survey of Generation Z in the United States, September 2021

"To marketers trying to convert me into a customer, I would have them look internally at the company that they are representing. I want to see companies like Ben & Jerry's who aren't afraid to speak up in times of discord."

—Rachel L.

"Instagram marketing is key. I have bought so many things from ads targeted at my interests."

—Hanalee M.

"Always be truthful in your message and use statistics to solidify your claims"... (Gen-Z hates dishonesty and loves organic missions). We also have a short attention span, so if marketing through video platforms like Instagram, TikTok and YouTube, keep it short and sweet! (Under 7 seconds):

Matilda M.

DID YOU KNOW?

The greatest online influencers in the lives of Gen Zers are their Gen Z friends.

34%: My Gen Z Friends
20%: Celebrities (Actors, Athletes, Musicians)
15%: Online Celebrities
11%: Subject Experts

Source: Mark Beal Survey of Generation Z in the United States, September 2021

"Just be genuine. Consumers can smell inauthentic pushes from brands – the market is inundated with that. Don't just put out a statement, put action behind it."

—Sarah M.

"My advice would be to be relatable and provide true value. I think it's also important to be conscious about the influencers selected to promote products, as it's easy to spot when someone is only promoting something for a paycheck versus when they actually are a fan of the product."

Julianna N.

"Be authentic. Customers can tell when brands are authentic and will hold them accountable when they are not in their words or actions."

—Frankie P.

"Having authentic brand purpose is the most important thing for growing your Gen Z customer base over the next decade."

—Michael P.

DID YOU KNOW?

Gen Z's favorite way to communicate visually is via Emojis (38%) followed by Memes (21%), GIFs (21%) and Bitmoji (16%)

Source: Mark Beal's Survey of Generation Z in the United States, September 2021

"We see through ads. I am going to want to invest in a product because it's good and people genuinely enjoy using it, not because you paid hundreds of thousands of dollars to create a fancy commercial."

—Sarah P.

"We want to be met where we're at in life and see that marketers care about the trends, issues, and stories that our generation is getting behind. As our interests evolve at a rapid pace, you have to start aligning your brand values to ours if you want to create brand loyalty."

—Alyssa R.

"Use your company's platform and reach to benefit and support causes outside of your brand."

—Roya R.

"Use influencers to share the brand and a real-life testimonial. We like, trust, and share the same interests as the influencers that we follow."

—Kylie R.

"We're constantly surrounded by products we 'need,' but brands that attempt to develop a personal connection with their consumers will always have the strongest customer base. Find your audience and understand who they are at their core – what makes them happy, what they support, why they support it, trends they're into and what aligns with their personality. Don't just try to sell them with all the bells and whistles because they can see right through that. Focus on making real, genuine connections and don't get complacent by thinking you have Gen Z all figured out – you don't."

—Shelby R.

"Tune into channels and interests that grab our tailored audience."

—Sydney R.

"Personalize your messaging and offer me a deal."

—Geno S.

"Being environmentally and socially responsible is a must. Other than those necessities, our generation values authenticity, transparency, and realness. By that, I mean we can see right through marketing jargon. We gravitate toward companies led by people who believe in their products, care for the people who work for them and also for those who consume their products."

—Hailley S.

"Is it Black-owned and sustainable?"

—Isaiah S.

"Be genuine, be honest, and do not make an NFT if you want to interest me in your products."

—Rebekah S.

"Make me a part of your community through engagement rather than simply selling me your product."

—Ryan S.

"Social media and celebrities/influencers that my generation follows are the best people you can reach out to help connect us with your brand."

—Samantha S.

"Be REAL with us. Authenticity is key and better received."

—Isabeau T.

"It's all about being and making an effort to connect with you rather than trying to change you."

—Rachel U.

"Be multi-dimensional."

—David W.

"I am most influenced by marketing ads that show me what makes their product different from the others on the market. This is especially influential when there are people around my age and similar interests that are using the product and give what at least seems to be an honest review about it."

—Nicole W.

"Have well-developed owned media channels. I love following businesses on social media with creative, organic, and relatable content that I can consume and then discuss with others. Not only using the platforms to promote products but the use of videos, TikTok's, Instagram Reels, etc to tell stories that aligns with the company's vision or brand. Additionally, promote sustainable content that contributes to the health of society. Businesses should embrace issues such as climate change and social inequality, by integrating authentic solutions into brands. Being aware of the environmental effects a company has is imperative. Businesses need to show they care about these issues which go beyond the brand. Not only is it good for business, but it's good for the world."

—Oliver W.

"Try to be different and set yourself apart. Make yourselves more attractive. One of the reasons I shop for clothes at Cotton On is because they are a sustainable brand and pay workers a fair wage. I like Taco Bell because they offer a plethora of vegetarian options that many fast food places don't. I would also throw away spokespeople. I am not going to Subway because Michael Strahan tells me too. I am not buying State Farm insurance because Baker Mayfield is promoting it. I think Gen Zers are getting smarter with spending their money."

—Nicholas Y.

Part IV

Recommendations for Employers

Recommendations for Employers

According to an October 12, 2021 article in *Fast Company*, Gen Z will comprise 30 percent of the workforce by 2030. If you are an employer, in just eight years, Generation Z employees will make up one third of your company. If you have not started to focus on recruiting and retaining Gen Z employees, this is the year to begin. With each passing year of graduation, tens of thousands of Gen Zers are making the transition from college to career, and they are seeking qualities, characteristics and benefits offered by an employer that no previous generation has prioritized.

Dishman, L. (2021, October 12). *Gen Z Job Seekers Are Finding Careers And Building Work Relationships In A Whole New Way*. Fast Company. Retrieved from https://www.fastcompany.com/90685254/gen-z-is-finding-jobs-and-building-relationships-in-a-whole-new-way

Beal, M. (2020, March 29). *COVID-19 Will Speed Up How Gen Z Transforms The World*. NJ.com. Retrieved from https://www.nj.com/opinion/2020/03/covid-19-will-speed-up-how-gen-z-transforms-the-world.html

Over the past several years I have conducted online surveys of Gen Zers in the United States regarding a variety of topics ranging from their favorite social media channels to areas of goal setting. I have explored their preferences when it comes to future employers. I ask members of this cohort questions regarding the most important qualities or characteristics they are seeking in future employers. Consistently, more than a third of Gen Zers claim that the most important quality they are seeking in a future employer is a corporate culture of diversity, equity and inclusion. While that may surprise some members of older generations who might have prioritized competitive salary and benefits, Gen Z is the most diverse and inclusive consumer segment in history. In my meetings with Gen Z, they express pride in being a member of the most diverse and inclusive generation. They wear it as a badge of honor and pride. It's a primary reason why they are seeking that same type of diversity and inclusion in the companies where they will ultimately work.

In March 2020, I authored a column in the *Newark Star Ledger* in which I proclaimed that the pandemic was expediting what Gen Z was going to usher in over the next decade – forcing companies to prioritize purpose over profits and inspiring employers to transform the way work gets conducted and completed. In September 2021, I surveyed Gen Zers nationwide and inquired about their preferred work location as they considered employers. Nearly a third (29%) claimed that having the ability to work a few days each week from home and a few days each week at an office would be the ideal situation while more than a quarter (27%) would like to work for an employer that empowers them to make their own decision where they would like to work. If Gen Z has to return to an office setting to work, nearly one-fifth (19%) claim that a safe and healthy office setting is their top priority while 15 percent are searching for office spaces that feature quiet rooms for mental health breaks and recharging.

In March 2020, COVID-19 unexpectedly ushered in an immediate transformation to working and the workplace that I believe would have slowly evolved over the next 10-20 years if a global pandemic had not arrived. Less than 18 months later, The Great Resignation ushered in a second transformation in which employees took control of their employment. Over the next decade, Gen Z will usher in a third transformation at the workplace by leveraging the advances and innovations that resulted from the pandemic and The Great Resignation. In my September 2021 survey of Gen Zers in the United States, nearly a quarter (23%) said they most identified with being an entrepreneur when provided a list of personas to select from. Another 11 percent consider themselves transformers and innovators according to my same survey.

Employers attempting to recruit and retain Gen Z must comprehend that Generation Z is not comprised of individuals simply interested in completing tasks. This generation is looking to challenge the status quo. They are eager to deliver measurable value to their employers via innovative and transformative solutions.

At the workplace, Gen Z wants to connect and collaborate in a diverse and inclusive corporate culture while being empowered. If an employer can't deliver that to Gen Z employees now and in the future, they will lose them as quickly as they hired them. If you don't believe me, read the quotes on the following pages from the Gen Zers who contributed to this book and offered their recommendations to employers.

DID YOU KNOW?

A corporate culture of diversity and inclusion (34%) is the top-quality Gen Zers are seeking in future employers followed by competitive salary (27%), competition benefits (24%), four-day work week (22%) and the ability to work from anywhere (13%).

Source: Mark Beal Survey of Generation Z in the United States, March 2021

"Flexibility is crucial. Companies can no longer say 'this job can't be done virtually.' The pandemic taught the world that we can successfully work from home. This is something that I will prioritize even more when I'm older and have children. I need to work for a company that can work with my busy life."

—Antonia A.

"Employees — especially Gen Z and Millennials — are realizing and demanding a shift in work culture, which has been accelerated by the pandemic. Workers want flexibility and for employers to not only accept but promote a strong work-life balance. This includes remote work options and competitive benefits (PTO, company perks, etc.). Additionally, organizations must realize the importance of diversity and inclusion and culture. Employees want to work for a company that offers a strong sense of community and recognizes the importance of different perspectives."

—Brian A.

"I thrive in a hybrid work environment that prioritizes company culture and work/life balance."

—Alexis B

"Being at a company who is willing to listen to the needs and the suggestions of the employees is paramount. Uplifting the morale of the people and providing fair compensation is how companies will retain top talent. Although culture has become a huge buzzword when applying to jobs, it genuinely is the aspect of a company that will set them apart from competitors. Feeling valued and appreciated at your job fuels employees and makes for an all-around productive and happier environment."

—Danielle B.

"Train, upscale, mentor, help in our development not just treating us as cogs in the machine. Have potential career paths or opportunities, not empty promises. If I feel like I can't grow there, then there's no future investment. When a company hardly gives out significant raises and cheats out long-term employees on pay, then I know they don't invest in their employees. As a manager, be loyal to your employees, and they'll be loyal to you. Invest in your employee and treat them well, and they'll do the same. It seems like companies and managers lose touch of their humanness in the midst of stress or their own goals. Our generation is so creative and resourceful – we can leave quickly for better opportunities, choose the gig economy, or build our own company from our side hustles if we don't feel fulfilled or treated well in our current job. I would say that most of the people I know in my generation want to be really passionate and connected to the work they do and the company that they represent. Recognize it's a two-way street. I am interviewing that company as much as they are interviewing me. Performative actions are easy to see through. Bad company culture can be quick to uncover. Companies are not in a vacuum and are made up of individuals who are impacted by social events, so companies need to recognize that. I want to know that my boss and company aligns genuinely supports and internally improves their DEI. I want to know that the company and management care for the wellbeing of their employees' mental health, work-life balance, and development."

—Layston B.

DID YOU KNOW?

Gen Zers most associate with the persona of the entrepreneur (23%), followed by activist (19%), collaborator/uniter (14%), transformer/innovator (11%) and amplifier/advocate (10%)

Source: Mark Beal Survey of Generation Z in the United States, September 2021

"I want an employer to respect my time off, have a hybrid (or at least flexible when needed) workplace and offer a truly competitive salary and benefits package with adequate time for recharging (not just competitive for the industry where the hourly wage breakdown is barely over minimum wage). Within the workplace, I want a company that wants my input, whether it be for company culture or bigger ideas for clients – even when I'm entry level. Ideally, the hierarchy that is present in so many companies would be spread out, rather than funnel up."

—Sam B.

"Create a hybrid environment. The workforce is changing, and it is no longer necessary for employees to be in the office daily. Rather than offering employees free coffee and lunches, consider offering mental and wellness days."

—Sean Bo.

DID YOU KNOW?

74% of Gen Zers rank purpose ahead of a paycheck when it comes to their employment.

Source: Knit (goknit.com)

"My advice to employers attempting to recruit and retain Gen Zers like me is to be constantly trying to improve upon office life, perks, and benefits. The traditional 9-5 and commuting every day to the office has been uprooted by COVID-19 and my generation isn't willing to go back to that. Work-life balance is the number one priority, with modern office cultures following close behind."

—Sean Bu.

"Listen to your employees; be consistent in seeking feedback from them. I think when employers are organized and stay on top of their employees' workload, their feedback, benefits, etc. employees are far more happy/engaged and willing to work harder. At this time, the two benefits that are the most important to me are health insurance and time off. I want to be able to feel comfortable with taking off for vacation, being sick and needing to call out, or taking off during an emergency. Without a doubt, there are employers who create environments where taking time off is discouraged. Due to the pandemic, I haven't had a lot of experience working in-person, but I love the idea of a hybrid workplace. I think it's important to feel connected to the place you're working for and I think being fully remote makes that difficult unless employers put in the effort to ensure employees don't feel alone or excluded. Diversity and inclusion are two aspects of work that I'm definitely seeing prioritized by more organizations. I think they should be prioritized by every workplace because how else do you expect your company to feel open and encouraging? Not only that, but by placing an importance on a diverse and inclusive workplace, you're able to bring more perspectives and experiences to the table, which is incredibly important in today's day and age."

—Brittany C.

DID YOU KNOW?

Nearly a third (29%) of Gen Zers believe a hybrid (2-3 Days Home/2-3 Days Office) work situation is the optimal way to work followed by the ability to decide where they work each week (27%), working remotely full-time (19%), working in an office full-time (13%) and working remotely and reporting to the office when needed for in-person meetings and collaboration (12%).

Source: Mark Beal Survey of Generation Z in the United States, September 2021

"Gen Z likes to be in control, or at least feel like they are. Giving them options that lets them dictate how they want to work will be crucial to recruitment and retention. For example, let future employees choose to work remote, or in-person. Another example could be giving them a selection of benefits and letting them choose which they would like."

—Carl C.

"To employers, I believe it is important to convey that the care for employees is at the top of the list when it comes to company values. To make sure that benefits for the employee and immediate family are offered and respected. With today's current climate, health, mental and physical, has been on the minds of many. The employer should make it known that employees are respected and not just another name on the company roster. When your employees are happy and healthy the company can only benefit, overall morale is the key to success."

—Gianna C.

DID YOU KNOW?

76% of Gen Zers describe themselves as responsible for driving their own careers.

Source: Knit (goknit.com)

"I think it is important to work for an employer who is willing to hear about employees' experiences and work practices in the workplace. Now that we have moved into a remote world, I think communicating with employees on a weekly or monthly basis is important to maintain employee inclusivity. I always appreciate it when my manager checks in with me just to check up on how I am doing (inside and outside of my work). It makes me feel included and that my company cares about my well-being, both in and outside of the office."

—Jenna C.

"COMPANY CULTURE!!!"

—Lara C.

"Employers should familiarize themselves with the extraordinary experiences that Gen Zers have gone through (ie. aftermath of 9/11, effects of the stock market crash, refugee crisis, COVID-19) and shape a company culture and work environment that provides employees the flexibility that they may need while also creating a new model of productivity for the business in this new digital age of society."

—Lauren C.

"In terms of recruiting employees, I would suggest that employers should continue to improve on campus recruitment at universities. Career fairs once a semester may be helpful to some, but a more individualized approach that I have seen to be more beneficial is targeting recruits through the Handshake platform. Retention may be a bit more difficult as I think Gen Z is always trying to find something bigger and better. Gen Z is always looking for the next pay raise or the next opportunity elsewhere rather than moving their way up at one company. Retention for this generation is incredibly important and I suggest that all employers should perform an end of the year evaluation. This would increase transparency among Gen Z and their employers. It will give them a sense of how they are doing, how they can improve, and how likely they may be to get a promotion or even what is required of them to attain that promotion. I know many Fortune 500 companies already perform these types of evaluations, but everyone deserves validation for their hard work, and everyone deserves to know if they are not performing as well as they should be."

—Margaret C.

"Purpose is a huge concept to me when it comes to considering an employer. As someone who enjoys receiving feedback on my work, I also like to be reminded what my purpose is and why I am spending over 40 hours a week committed to one company or project. I find that anyone in my generation is looking for our purpose, both personally and professionally, so being shown appreciation and gratitude by a company goes a long way; otherwise, we will look for a company who does show that we have purpose."

Ashley D.

"The COVID-19 pandemic has taught us that we can still be productive -- sometimes even more productive -- when working from home. There are many ways to boost morale and encourage corporate culture without being confined to our cubicles."

—Jenna D.

"The biggest piece of advice I give to employers attempting to recruit and retain Gen Z is to put transparency at the forefront of company messaging and culture, specifically with regards to compensation, job expectations and advancement for all roles. If companies are transparent about the previously mentioned topics, they are more likely to find and retain candidates that better fit what they are looking for. Additionally, it is incredibly important to me that a company's messaging strongly aligns with the actions taken by senior management. If a company is frequently posting on social media about how their culture emphasizes a strong work/life balance, this should also be reflected in the company's day-to-day operations with its employees."

—Jennifer D.

DID YOU KNOW?

Gen Z is looking for the following if required to return to work in an office setting:

19%: Safe & Healthy Office Setting
18%: Assigned Office/Desk Space
17%: Free Snacks/Beverages
15%: Quiet Rooms For Mental Breaks/Recharge
12%: Open Office Setting/No Assigned Seating
10%: Consistent Advances In Office Technology

Source: Mark Beal Survey of Generation Z in the United States, September 2021

"I find corporate social responsibility to be one of the best things a company can focus on today. There's lots of activism going on and people want to work for companies that share their values and work towards the same goals. CSR is not only a great way to recruit employees but also a way to positively impact the world."

—Joelle D.

"We have proven that we can either work or be educated in a work/learn from home environment. Employers must be flexible in that aspect of working. If any generation is capable of working from home, it is Gen Z. We are no longer working in a society that needs to be in a physical office 9-5 or longer five days a week. Gen Z wants work/ life balance."

—Summer D.

"The work environment of a company is an important element to consider when deciding to take a job. I don't believe most of Gen Z wants to work for a company that is extremely high stress and shows little empathy and human emotion for their employees. When considering starting a career somewhere, I want to feel confident that I am joining a team of like-minded people that value each other for more than just the numbers and results of their work. Having leadership that possesses emotional intelligence and values the creation of a positive and supportive work environment is very important."

—Troy D.

"Prioritize work life balance."

—Cristina F.

"Each year, there are multiple trends that drive workplace culture. My advice to future employers is to be aware of what is important to young people entering the workplace and combine that with your company's morals. Valuing the employee and providing them with an environment where they can express and push themselves is what will drive company success and satisfied workers."

—Gabrielle F.

"Wellness and health benefits are becoming more common. It empowers employees to live healthy and focus on themselves throughout their busy lives. This in return positively affects the overall environment and productiveness of the workplace."

—Olivia F.

"Be flexible, but not too flexible. Definitely offer full time remote and hybrid work environments where employees can choose what work dynamic/environment is best for them. Provide more PTO (not unlimited because that creates a slippery slope of not using it or using it too much) and make them use it. Provide one companywide Monday off every other month for mental health. Allow employees to flex their hours so they can work longer in order to get off earlier in the week. Have more weekly/bi-weekly companywide Zoom calls to have a sandbox environment safe space to talk freely about any ranging sensitive topics. Send monthly/bi-monthly care packages to your employees to show them that they are more than just a number, that they matter, and that you are appreciative of their time, effort, and livelihood. Encourage employees to take breaks throughout the day to make work less nonstop, more interesting, etc. Schedule calls among c-suites and company teams more often, like at least once every other month. Overall, be more understanding, empathetic, and accommodating to your employees and their needs."

—Adam G.

"Employers have to stop living in the past. We are in the now, we as employees are adjusted to work from home or hybrid work. We want to feel supported, not watched. We want to feel empowered, not controlled. Promote the best performers and do not make excuses as to why you can't reach their salary expectations. When an employee is brave enough to speak up about a culture or management issue, listen carefully and create tactical next steps to remedy these concerns or risk losing your best talent. My generation now realizes the power is in our hands (at least for now) and the pandemic has taught us how precious our time is – we won't waste it begging employers to treat and pay us fairly, we'll leave for another company that will or we'll start our own."

—Katie G.

"Employers must be upfront, straight to the point, and offer benefits that are exclusive to said company. They need to have answers to both present and future questions that offer excitement, security, and growth."

—Paris G.

"Traditional ways of operating such as a strict 9-5, working full time in a physical office, or a strict dress code are hallmarks of traditional professionalism, but many in Gen Z view these practices as too restrictive or unnecessary. The culture is changing and for employers to successfully hire and retain staff from the Gen Z, considering changes to traditional office culture may be their best strategy."

—Pat G.

"Develop a more relaxed company culture in behavior, dress, and environment. I personally find a more laid-back culture where employees feel comfortable, can laugh, and be real people to be appealing. I don't like the idea of having to come into work in a suit and tie every day, nor do I like the idea of sitting in a gray cubicle for a full eight hours. Create an office space that is stimulating, creative, and interesting. Work should feel fun!"

—Alessandra I.

"As there are signs of a safe environment to work in the years to come, employers should push for in-person work as business has always and will always be built upon face-to-face interactions, at least for the foreseeable future. A person can get a message across much more clearly and strongly when they have their emotions and charisma to back the message, rather than saying it in a Zoom call or sending it over email. However, there should still be flexibility for remote work if appropriate and practical for each work situation/profession in case uncertain situations take place from the ongoing pandemic. This also leads to flexibility in work location if remote work is called for as the primary form of work for a certain company."

—Ryan J.

"We need to be paid more. Entry-level jobs out of college should not pay the same amount as high-school positions or those that do not require a degree. I may be young, but I know my worth and my worth is more than $15 an hour."

—Gillian K.

"Gen Z employees are the cream of the crop, in my opinion. We have everything a future employer could want: the grasp of social media, the technical skills, the openness for change, and the willingness to get the job done as quickly and efficiently as possible. I think as a generation, Gen Z has taken the advice from the older generations and found ways to complete tasks more efficiently (with technology) that some older generations may be more intimidated by."

—Hannah K.

"Allows remote work when possible, in addition to in-person."

—Kayla L.

DID YOU KNOW?

42% of Gen Zers said they want to have their own business (10 percentage points hire than all other working generations surveyed).

Source: Knit (goknit.com)

"I'm interested in companies that treat their employees fairly: fair wages, time off, as well as benefits, as well as prioritizing the mental health of your employees. I'd also be more inclined to work for a company that has solid morals and will stand up to injustices 365 days of the year, not when pressured to."

—Kymani L.

"Strike a balance with salary and mission. People are no longer just 1) chasing checks or 2) forgoing pay for free beer."

—Micah L.

"I will always prefer a workplace where I can work remotely and save myself a commute. My work life balance has completely transformed since I began working remotely in March 2020, and I value that time saved to the point where I do not mind committing the time I would have spent commuting to working. It seems like a win/win for employee and employer."

—Rachel L.

"Stop requiring five years of experience for entry level positions. Something my generation doesn't lack is motivation. Employers should have greater flexibility to work from home and I prefer a work culture that is inclusive and fun. I think formal attire is a thing of the past and more companies should be open to casual attire."

—Hanalee M.

"Like Patagonia, include your mission and passion with every marketing campaign. Once Gen Z recognizes that your genuine, they will want to work for you."

—Matilda M.

"You need to ensure that you support your employees. Pizza parties and cool offices are great - but employees that feel supported for work-life balance, learning and development, etc. are the ones that will stay. Those are the real important things."

—Sarah M.

"I think it's important for employers to be conscious of their future employees' personal lives, and the new world we are living in today when attempting to recruit. The option to work remotely has been proven to be effective within the last two years, and there is no reason to go back to mandatory in office days at this point. I think it is also important for them to recognize that inflation has dramatically increased, and minimum wage is just not acceptable for 20-somethings with student loan debt and astronomical rent costs."

—Julianna N.

"Build morale, don't break it. Company culture is the foundation for strong relationships in the workplace."

—Frankie P.

"Gen Zers want to work for brands that are truly doing good for the world. If we aren't passionate about your brand's mission and purpose, we're not going to work for you."

—Michael P.

DID YOU KNOW?

91% of Gen Z said they are more likely to take a job at a company that is socially conscious.

Source: Knit (goknit.com)

"Flexibility and the ability to do multiple things is at the core of what I do, and I know I'm not the only person who feels that way. You have to respect that because, when you do, you're actually going to get the best work out of us. We know there's more to life than sitting behind a desk for nine hours a day in a cubicle for minimum wage. We aren't afraid to test your loyalty to us. COVID has affected most of Gen Z's adult life, and it's given us a lot of clarity and perspective."

—Sarah P.

"We want structure, but freedom to grow and want to work at a company whose workplace culture, values our differences in areas of race, gender, sexuality, and expertise."

—Alyssa R.

"Providing tools (i.e. technology, office furniture) to work from home is still required because there are graduates that come out of college (in a pandemic) who cannot afford certain technology/office space and are expected to perform at the same level as everyone else. Along with financial aid for necessities, employees should offer all types of benefits including commutation, health insurance, 401k plans and relocation assistance."

—Flor R.

"Create and maintain a workplace that cares about our wellbeing. It's important that the workplace is psychologically and emotionally healthy environment."

—Kylie R.

DID YOU KNOW?

Gen Z's preferred way to communicate at work is email (33%) followed by text/direct message (26%), Discord (15%), Google Hangouts (11%), Teams/Zoom (9%) and Slack (6%).

Source: Mark Beal Survey of Generation Z in the United States, September 2021

"A hybrid work structure is a wonderful benefit that companies should continue to utilize permanently. This permits employees to have the flexibility to determine their remote/in-person schedule and allows them the freedom to pursue other hobbies and interests outside of work during the time they might have spent commuting, which in turn can improve their well-being and overall morale."

—Roya R.

"Offer employees the opportunity to work where they will be the most productive. The pandemic showed us how we can still get down to business when working remotely and your employees want to know you trust them to fulfill their job requirements without constant supervision. Be the type of boss that you wish you had in the early stages of your career. People don't often quit bad jobs, they quit bad management – which can be avoided by providing a safe and welcoming environment that prioritizes humanity over profit."

—Shelby R.

"Take a chance on me, because I will make a difference."

—Sydney R.

"Treat us well. Great pay and benefits should only be the start."

—Geno S.

DID YOU KNOW?

71% of Gen Zers agree that working full-time from home is acceptable.

Source: Mark Beal Survey of Generation Z in the United States, September 2021

"Above all else, we need to raise the bar when it comes to corporate culture. We need to cultivate collaborative environments with engaging work - especially with remote work being something that is here to stay. We need to feel like our work matters in order feel fulfilled and that the people we work with and for, care about us. Some ways to ensure include offering mental health PTO days, real life-work balance, achievable KPIs, and flexible work location and hours."

—Hailley S.

"The job must be remote WFH (work from home) with full salary benefits and unlimited PTO with paid sabbatical leave."

—Isaiah S.

"It is essential to offer remote work as a supplement or replacement for an in-person environment, because not only does it allow for people to have more control over their flow and productivity, but it helps preserve mental health. Employers must be cognizant of the toll of the pandemic on everything, then reflect that in their wages or benefits. 2020 has especially shown the progress we've yet to make in diversity and inclusion, meaning that an authentic approach to this must happen to better address humanity at large, rather than just from the interests of employers."

—Rebekah S.

DID YOU KNOW?

LinkedIn is one of the preferred content channels of older Gen Zers. Here is how they are utilizing the platform.

32%: Searching For Jobs/Internships
30%: Networking & Making Career Connections
12%: Sharing Thought Leadership Content
10%: Reading Thought Leadership Content
10%: Following Career Achievements Of Friends
7%: Learn Of Best Companies To Work For

Source: Mark Beal Survey of Generation Z in the United States, September 2021

"Make sure your needs and my needs intertwine. Our priorities should not be competing, but rather in concert."

—Ryan S.

"Remote work is the way to go for my generation right now. We are young, eager to travel, and don't want to be around the stereotypical lifestyle of living with your parents (even though deep down we will be thankful for this in the long run)."

—Samantha S.

"If you take pride in your diversity and inclusion efforts in the workplace, please make sure these efforts are genuine and ongoing."

—Isabeau T.

"Corporate culture says a lot about how the company is run. Listening to your employees and what they have to say can be beneficial to the organization. An individual's title or role in the company does not define their skill level or knowledge of the subject at hand."

—Rachel U.

"Be flexible, friendly, and most importantly, prioritize mental health."

—David W.

"What I value most as an employee is an environment of mutual respect and trust, a healthy work/life balance and personal and professional growth opportunities. When I evaluate potential companies to work for, I look for a purpose that is being served and a product that I can believe in and fully support. I do not wish to work for a company with poor leadership or lack of morals."

—Nicole W.

"The future of employment depends on the industry and job. Certain jobs may offer a large variety of benefits. It is extremely attractive when employers invest in their employees. As an employee, it's important to feel appreciated. I have never worked in an office, but I find it enticing when companies offer the option to work remotely. It provides the employee more responsibility and freedom to live where they want."

—Oliver W.

"Give employees what they want. Pay your workers a fair wage. The world is changing. People desire flexibility. A work/ life balance is critical for happiness and productivity. Hybrid or remote offices are going to be critical. Young people want their time back. To get young people to work labor jobs, their needs to be more incentive. Paying a 20-year-old $2.31 an hour before tips to serve food to rude and ungrateful customers who demean and demoralize young people for their appetizers taking too long is why restaurants, for example, have such a high turnover rate. Make it worth it."

—Nicholas Y.

Part V

Insights
on Societal Issues

Insights
on Societal Issues

Generation Z is the 'Purpose Generation.' They are looking to become customers of brands and employees of companies that prioritize purpose. An *Ad Age* study reported that 69 percent of Gen Zers are more likely to purchase from companies that contribute to social causes.

Gen Z is actively conducting research to learn how companies responded to the Black Lives Matter awakening and the global pandemic. In my September 2021 survey of Gen Z, more than 90 percent claim they conduct some research before purchasing a product to learn if the company or brand has acted purposefully. Acting with purpose could include a company's support of charities, their impact on the environment and their response to societal issues.

Dugan, M. E. (2019, April 15). *Gen Z Doesn't Want To Buy Your Brand, They Want To Join It.* Ad Age. Retrieved from https://adage.com/article/wp-engine/gen-z-doesnt-want-buy-your-brand-they-want-join-it/2163281

Societal issues including social justice, mental health and the environment are important to this generation. It's one of the reasons why Patagonia is among the brands that this generation loves. As noted earlier, Patagonia's mission to, "save our home planet" is the purpose-led approach that engages Gen Z.

Mental health, once a taboo topic, is of utmost importance to Gen Z. In my September 2021 survey of Gen Z, nearly 40 percent (37%) of Gen Zers said that mental health is their top goal-setting area compared to physical health, financial wellness and professional development. When we look back 15-20 years from now, I believe Generation Z will receive the credit for transforming mental health into a mainstream conversation in school, at work and in popular culture that will never go away. They will encourage more employers to offer mental health benefits including mental health days. I believe we will also see more companies and brands make mental health the centerpiece of future campaigns and programs after being inspired and informed by Gen Z.

If you don't believe me and my predictions, read the words directly from the minds and mouths of the oldest members of the 'Purpose Generation' as it relates to societal issues including mental health and the environment.

DID YOU KNOW?

Mental health is the top setting goal area for Gen Z.
37%: Mental Health
27%: Physical Health
27%: Financial Wellness
10%: Professional Development

Source: Mark Beal Survey of Generation Z in the United States, September 2021

Mental Health/Wellness: "I prioritize health and wellness immensely. Both physically and mentally it is crucial to take care of yourself and others around you."

—Antonia A.

Mental Health: "Companies must realize the prioritization of mental health by their employees — the pandemic, specifically, has shined a light on mental health. An organization recognizing the importance of mental health and wellbeing isn't limited to offering mental health resources, for example. Instead, employees' wellbeing — at least in the context of work — is shaped by the whole package that a company offers: work flexibility, hours, benefits, culture, and overall employee satisfaction."

—Brian A.

Education: "It is critical for employers to encourage and support employees who are eager to continue their education."

—Alexis B.

Environment: "*Companies need to be environmentally conscious and recognize both the impact and the opportunity of sustainability. Being in the beauty industry, I see significant waste, so witnessing brands starting to prioritize recycled materials and introducing refillable packaging is really exciting. It's important that companies lead by example and consumers do so as well so we can minimize waste and look towards a more environmentally responsible future.*"

—Danielle B.

Healthcare: "*Distilling it to one is hard. I feel like I live in a dystopia when we have to fight for basic human rights: universal healthcare, women's reproductive rights, and for the POC and Black Lives Matter movement. It seems criminal that someone would lose their healthcare when they lose their job. The fact that so many people were laid off during a global pandemic and left without healthcare insurance is apocalyptic. Universal healthcare, particularly across states, would improve healthcare access. America is incredibly backwards for not having universal healthcare and that it isn't treated bipartisan. We are the only country in the developed world without it.*"

—Layston B.

Purpose: "I have found that I thrive in a workplace when I feel purpose in what I am doing and feel that the impact of my work matters. When the company I am working for recognizes that, feeds into my strengths and makes me feel important, that is when I am most successful and therefore the company is most successful. I feel that when you support internally, the larger group rises above the rest."

—Sam B.

Education: "Educating our society is incredibly important and can be done outside the classroom. Organizations and corporations should further employees' knowledge and provide resources to develop life-long learners."

—Sean Bo.

Purpose: "I think everyone in Generation Z has their causes that they support, and most of which are very noble. However, one thing that I think my generation can agree upon is that there is life beyond work. We seek a strong, non-toxic work culture as well as a balance between life and work. Our generation isn't afraid to leave companies that don't conform to that standard either, especially in an era of innovation like what we were raised in."

—Sean Bu.

Environment: "If we don't work to help our planet, we won't have a healthy, safe environment to live. Watching species go extinct, seeing pollution all around the world, hearing about people becoming sick because they live in polluted areas is very upsetting. I remember when the pandemic initially hit and the entire world was in lockdown, we saw dolphins in the Venice Canal waters, noise pollution went down, CO2 emissions dropped, animal sightings increased. It was all so encouraging, and I think it really proved we need to do something to make sure this planet stays as healthy as it can. The importance of the environment has even impacted where I shop, knowing how many brands are fast-fashion, use sweatshops, and are renowned plastic polluters."

—Brittany C.

Mental Health: "Mental Health is very important to me. I have been fortunate enough to not struggle with mental health issues, but I have a family history of mental health issues along with many good friends who have suffered through anxiety and depression. I always look toward the companies who support mental health strongly."

—Carl C.

Mental Health: "I feel that Mental Health is one that I can personally speak on. I've been dealing with anxiety and depression for quite some time but came to about five years ago. My journey has not been easy, but to my surprise, the more I speak on my experiences with friends, family, and even strangers, I am reminded how everyone deals with some sort of anxiety and dark times now and again. It has become increasingly easier to share experiences and speak out on the matter, especially since the pandemic."

—Jenna C.

Education: "Education is the most imperative of society to invest in... offering a more level playing field to all youth which could help with several ongoing macro-issues."

—Lara C.

Diversity & Inclusion: "More often than not, diversity and inclusion efforts within companies tend to ignore the complexities that this phrase depicts, but by listening to the different communities that affect the successes of each company, the culture of creating a more diverse and inclusive environment can be achieved."

—Lauren C.

Mental Health: "A societal issue that is not talked about often enough among our generation in college is the anxiety that we face when interviewing for internships or full-time positions. Very frequently on LinkedIn, we see all of our classmates and peers posting amazing new job offers and acceptances, and that can lead to anxiety among many students who feel as though they are not as far along in the process."

—Margaret C.

Purpose: "We can use our voices and our words to do so many things. Using them to do good and inspire change is what fulfills me. It's why I look up to companies prioritizing purpose-driven communications."

—Jenna D.

Mental Health: "While there are so many societal issues in the world that deserve attention and recognition, the one that is most important to me is mental health. Mental illness is something that goes unnoticed by most on a daily basis, and since the start of the COVID-19 pandemic, the mental health crisis we face has only worsened. For this reason, I think it's so important that individuals struggling with their mental health have options available to them, such as counseling, therapy sessions, and medication, at a *reasonable* cost."

—Jennifer D.

Mental Health: "Mental Health has been so stigmatized, and that stigma really makes it difficult for people to find the strength to seek treatment. Thankfully, there is more of a focus and a push for people to seek help today than there was when my parents were young and that is so important. I am very open about my mental health just because I think people need to know that they are not alone and mental health struggles are not something to be ashamed of. There is still some stigma and that needs to stop."

—Joelle D.

DID YOU KNOW?

91% of Gen Zers will research a company before purchasing its products to confirm the company is purposeful in their actions and the way in which they conduct business.

Source: Mark Beal Survey of Generation Z in the United States, September 2021

Mental Health: "Gen Z is definitely the most open when it comes to mental health. We witnessed at the Olympic Games in 2021, Simone Biles, the top gymnast in the world, taking herself out of the competition due to mental health issues. We are not afraid to resign from a job, be open about seeing a therapist or need help from prescriptions for anxiety or depression like past generations were. I know many people my age who have left a job due to the climate of the office or the workload that was put on them being the 'lowest level' employee. This does not mean we are lazy or do not want to work, but instead we know our worth and want to work for a company that sees that and respects us as one of their employees."

—Summer D.

Diversity & Inclusion: "It is human nature to be able to adapt to the environment you are in. However, when it comes to workplace culture, it is crucial to ensure you are in a space where you are surrounded by people who embrace different perspectives and value the importance of inclusivity."

—Gabrielle F.

Mental Health: "Mental Health is something that often gets overlooked in the workplace. Companies should provide free mental health services for their employees. This could include therapy and psychiatric services."

—Olivia F.

DID YOU KNOW?

89% of Gen Z said they are more likely to purchase products from companies that support charitable causes.

Source: Knit (goknit.com)

Mental Health: "Having a creative outlet such as music has kept me sane while working long hours at an agency. Regardless of how crazy work may get, my passion has kept me fulfilled and has helped me avoid burnout."

—Cristina F.

Environment: "Look at the news not only in the United States but across the world. There are so many massive environmental health crises going on every week. From tornados, severe drought and flooding, hurricanes, to even volcanic eruptions. We are witnessing some of the most irregular and extreme weather ever, and it's only going to continue to get worse as anthropogenic effects heighten as time moves on and no legislation/initiatives are taken to reverse such damage we are doing to the earth. If this topic is given more attention, less people will be struggling and facing the consequences, there will be more jobs created to help reverse anthropogenic climate change, and the world will be a better place to live for generations to come. Earth and its health is the single most important issue of society in my opinion, and if it's addressed, I believe it will help heal other major issues and trigger a domino effect of solutions to them as well."

—Adam G.

Mental Health: "*Mental health struggles have become the silent killer of my generation, especially as we continue to fight the pandemic. I'm hopeful that my generation can redirect the way we use social media and other forms of digital connection – to remove constant comparison and bullying to make way for a more communal space. If these platforms are going to be part of our lives forever, we have to find a way to make them uplifting, less addictive, and based in authenticity. By sharing our own struggles with mental health (whether online or in person), we give others the courage to speak their truth. I've found this almost always creates a space for healing and togetherness, something I think we need more than ever as a generation.*"

—Katie G.

Purpose: "When looking at the current state of our society, I believe we have a lot of underlying issues contributing to the lack of our attention span. We crave knowledge in the immediate, while lacking the patience in taking the time to read more into trending topics and headlines. The world is moving faster than the human mind can comprehend. This is due to the technological advancements in the digital world we live in. We need to be reminded what it means to be human and take time to gather our thoughts while coming to educated conclusions when relating to issues like cultural advancement, equality, environmental protection, politics, foreign relations, and other present topics that affect our daily lives."

—Paris G.

Mental Health: "Gen Z is highly focused on societal issues and finding ways to support them. Personally, I think mental health is very important and it is something that is becoming increasingly addressed from both brands and employers."

—Pat G.

Environment: "Environmental destruction is going to be the next disaster after COVID-19, and it currently is. We all just don't know it yet because not everyone is facing its dire effects. I believe environmental impact to be very important because without this Earth, what can we do? Brands should do better to implement real measures that refrain from exhausting our planet's resources, polluting, and destroying ecosystems."

—Alessandra I.

Environment: "Issues surrounding the environment and ways to maintain sustainability on local, corporate, and agricultural levels should be incorporated more into education at all levels. These topics are already being acted upon by multiple industries and will only grow in the future so information about them needs to be taught to younger generations in order to nurture innovative strategies to deal with them."

—Ryan J.

DID YOU KNOW?

When asked to think of a brand they believe to be socially conscious, 18% of Gen Zers said, Patagonia.

Source: Knit (goknit.com)

Environment: "The power that corporations hold against the environment is not to be taken lightly. While it is not lawfully a company's responsibility to make the environment a better place, I believe that because of the impact that large companies have on the environment, they should be held accountable for their waste, pollution, and where their products end up regardless of consumer behavior."

—Gillian K.

Mental Health: "One societal issue that is important to me is mental health. I think as a generation we have fully changed the narrative on mental health, and we still have a lot more to go. Older generations suffered from the silence on the topic, and I have seen it affect people in my personal life. As an individual, it means the most to me because changing the narrative has truly changed people's lives that I know and my own."

—Hannah K.

Mental Health: "You'll never feel 100% ready."

—Kayla L.

Mental Health: "I'm an advocate for mental health awareness, especially among my generation because it is something that isn't as prioritized as it should be, and there are still some lingering stigmas surrounding it that prevent people from getting the help they need."

—Kymani L.

Purpose: "As Johnson & Johnson puts it, "Health for Humanity." All causes are intertwined and deserve attention."

—Micah L.

Mental Health: "The stigma around mental health, while diminished, is not gone. I see myself valuing companies - whether to work at or engage with - who value their employees' mental health as a primary concern. I would rather purchase from a company that I know prioritizes about the mental health of their employees than a company who does not."

—Rachel L.

Mental Health: "I value mental health. I am very open about my journey and my recovery from an eating disorder after spending a month in rehab in 2020."

—Hanalee M.

DID YOU KNOW?

What Gen Z is looking for when researching companies before making a purchase?
22%: Company Is Environmentally Friendly
22%: Company Supports Charities Important To Gen Z
19%: Company Acted Purposefully In Response To Black Lives Matter & COVID
16%: Company Is Diverse & Inclusive

Source: Mark Beal Survey of Generation Z in the United States, September 2021

Diversity & Inclusion: "Recognizing companies excel when they foster inclusion and embrace diversity is how you can stand out from the competitors."

—Matilda M.

Mental Health: "Mental health isn't just a fad for companies to say they support. It is important to actually find ways to support employees with mental illness and those who need mental health breaks. In recent years it seems to have become a trend, and while it's great that it is being spotlighted and talked about - the reality of the issue cannot be diminished."

—Sarah M.

Mental Health: "Mental Health is extremely important to me, especially as a 25-year-old in such a transitional era of my life—that just so happens to be occurring during one of the most 'unprecedented' times we've seen in decades. Adjusting to the responsibilities and expectations that come with adulthood is especially difficult when literally no one in the world knows what they're doing right now. I think mental health is something everyone should be conscious of, especially those that are experiencing the same transitions in life as I am. Remember that it's okay to put yourself first sometimes—you can't put on someone's oxygen mask if you don't put your own on first. Find a good work-life balance and find happiness in everything you do."

—Julianna N.

DID YOU KNOW?

Just over 30% of Gen Zers believe that only 5-10% of companies are socially conscious.

Source: Knit (goknit.com)

Purpose: *"People are quick to criticize 'cancel culture.' But when you reframe it as accountability culture — something elementary school teachers attempt to instill in children — you realize that the ability and willingness to improve is the big thing my generation generally values: improving justice for all, giving everyone a chance to be heard and evaluating systems that should work better. We are looking to contribute progress, not conserve old ways of doing things that don't work for most."*

—Sarah P.

Mental Health: *"Mental health impacts our thoughts, emotions, and behaviors. It affects our day-to-day activities such as school, work, and relationships with others which is why it is so important to acknowledge the importance of good mental health efforts. As Gen Zers, most of us are open to talking about mental health and aren't afraid to advocate for ourselves/others to break stigma and raise awareness."*

—Kylie R.

Diversity: "When we start to see that diversity is a blessing rather than something to be wary of and incorporate people of color and members of diverse communities (race, gender, sexuality, social-economic, etc.) into the workplace, we'll start to see success in every area of the job. Embracing diversity means embracing inclusivity and ensures that when you're marketing, your organization is creating content that is appropriate across every culture and background."

—Alyssa R.

Purpose: "I believe a company's purpose should go above and beyond their respective products or services. The most purposeful companies understand the magnitude of their reach and influence and utilize them in ways that benefit not only themselves but the community as a whole."

—Roya R.

Mental Health: "The current labor movement that we are experiencing demonstrates that employees want to know their employers care about their well-being. We've collectively experienced tremendous loss over the past few years and people are tired of working themselves to the bone for companies that wouldn't bat an eye to replace them. Mental health days, in my opinion, should be included in all PTO benefits. We aren't machines, we can't always be running on empty. We need time to rest and recharge to avoid burnout so we can perform at our best."

—Shelby R.

Mental Health: "The importance of mental health is now more vital than ever as the constant online interaction is at an all-time high."

—Sydney R.

Purpose: "I should never have to defend why I work at an organization."

—Geno S.

Environment: "The planet needs our help NOW and there is only so much an individual can do to reduce their carbon footprint. Companies have an obligation to reduce their carbon emissions to enact REAL change in a serious way."

—Hailley S.

Mental Health: "It's time for the four-day work week."

—Isaiah S.

Mental Health: *"I think there needs to be an awakening for the conversation around mental health as a society. We made these rigid initial parameters to shut out those with disabilities, then opened up the floodgates to everyone when the virus hit. By extension, mental health directly correlates with some of these other points, because a happier person will feel more inclined to engage in community, contribute to their sense of purpose, and, if they are treated as a complete being, their mental health may improve."*

—Rebekah S.

Purpose: *"Never get so busy making a living that you forget to make a life."*

—Ryan S.

Diversity & Inclusion: *"Efforts around DE&I are key to making the workplace feel less toxic, more engaging and overall, to retain employees. The more we can talk about our experiences, the more we can understand each other and break down the corporate wall of privilege."*

—Isabeau T.

Purpose: *"If you don't have a purpose in what you're doing, then you're just going through the motions rather than making an impact."*

—Rachel U.

"Mental health is important to me because it is never addressed enough in the world. More people have to know about mental health, and this allows for more people to open up!"

—David W.

Purpose: "I appreciate companies that are purpose-driven as they appear more authentic and innovative. I am more loyal to a company that has a purpose in society and that is consistent with its values. Global businesses have platforms in which they can promote change and solutions. They are also the businesses that use the most resources which is why creating a purpose is essential to growing business to the next generation."

—Oliver W.

Mental Health: "I think mental health is really important. We live in a digital age now. We're living through a pandemic. Humans are more open than ever, and mental health needs to be prioritized. If you're constantly burnt out, depressed, exhausted or anxious because of work, then you never truly unplug."

—Nicholas Y.

Part VI

Aspirations:
Where Gen Z Wants
To Be In A Decade

Aspirations: Where Gen Z Wants To Be In A Decade

In 2021, I was presenting my Gen Z research, insights and implications to a group of marketers. During the concluding question and answer session of my presentation, one marketer asked if I knew where Generation Z would be in a decade. Would they still be the 'Purpose Generation' or would the responsibilities of adulthood – career, marriage, children and home ownership - change their focus and perspective? I was stumped. For the first time that I could recall, I did not have an answer to a question regarding Generation Z. It was that question and my inability to answer it that was an inspiration for this book. It is also the focus of this final section.

As part of my survey of the oldest members of Gen Z, my final question asked them about their goals and aspirations for the next decade. Where did the senior members of Gen Z want to be in 10 years professionally, personally or both?

Some Gen Zers were transparent and said they could not answer the question at this time as they were just starting the first chapter of their career. Others focused exclusively on their professional life while others shared personal aspirations regarding family and children.

As you read the words of Generation Z on the following pages, I hope you are inspired as I am. As I read about their dreams, goals and aspirations, I was infused with optimism and hope. They share a glimpse into the journey they will take over the next decade, a journey that goes beyond themselves as individuals. Themes which have already been introduced in this book are shared again – passion, innovation, transformation, entrepreneurism and purpose. I interpreted their aspirations as selfless rather than selfish. They included references to communities and family and helping others.

I believe the future of the world is bright and in good hands as Generation Z takes the baton from previous generations and assumes leadership roles in neighborhoods, communities, schools, companies and organizations of all sizes. I am confident that over the next decade and beyond, Gen Z will make the world a better place than the one into which they were born.

"In the next 10 years I hope to establish myself in a career that I am passionate about, that changes people's lives for the better and that I am successful in. Once I am established in my career, I hope to travel more, buy a house, get married and start a family."

—Antonia A.

"The next decade will bring me to my mid-30s. Professionally, I hope to garner more experience in high-stakes communications — political, corporate, agency — and earn a senior-level role where my impact would be greatest. Personally, I hope to be a homeowner and continue my valued relationships with friends and family."

—Brian A.

"I hope to be a financially stable homeowner who can provide for her husband and children while working full-time in a senior marketing manager role."

—Alexis B.

"I never knew customer success existed until I fell into it in my current role at a tech company. Now I absolutely love this facet of business and I am so excited to continue pursuing my career in it. I feel so lucky to be in the tech world as many positions, especially in customer success, are extremely coveted. I am so grateful to be in this role for my first job because I know it will catapult me into a very successful future in an industry that is constantly evolving. I don't know what I will achieve in 10 years, but I do know I am always open to learning and excited to be agile alongside the tech industry."

—Danielle B.

"I would love to either be or still on the journey to be financially free. I plan to become a coach - whether it be a career or financial coach with personalized workshops. I would like to live abroad again because it's good to go beyond the America-only perspective."

—Layston B.

"My biggest goal in the next decade is to grow – I want to break barriers and succeed in my career, grow my family and, above all, I hope to be the happiest I've ever been."

Sam B.

"In the next ten years, I hope to develop my own corporation that is viewed as highly ethical and adaptable to the ongoing changes in our society."

—Sean Bo.

"My goals and aspirations are ambiguous, because I don't know where life will take me. That being said, I do have a foundation of goals that I want to achieve. I want to achieve financial security and freedom. I want to achieve genuine happiness in my life, and I want to find a cause, or causes, to really devote myself to and focus on. These three things are of the utmost importance in not just my life, but I believe in the lives of those from my generation as well."

—Sean Bu.

"Within the next 10 years, I'd like to be thriving in my career field and reach a point where I can buy a house without anyone's help. Two of the most important values I have are working hard and being independent. I've been this way since I was 16 and now that I'm 25, I find myself setting bigger goals for myself and my future: secure a promotion before the typical time frame, buy a home, earn a six-figure salary by 30."

—Brittany C.

"Over the next decade, I hope to be effectively representing and marketing a pro sports organization such as the National Football League or National Basketball Association."

—Carl C.

"My aspirations for the next decade are to never underestimate my potential and go for roles that hold power within my department as I continue to grow within the company. To always remember that through my hard work and persistent attitude I have opened many doors within my career. Success to me is a balance of being happy within my personal and professional life, and to always remember to have fun in what I am doing. Who says work can't be fun?"

—Gianna C.

"In the next 10 years, I hope I am able to pinpoint my passion in life. I have some ideas about the things that inspire me, but I am having trouble putting the pieces together to find exactly what it is I want to do in life--personally and professionally. After graduating from university, it occurred to me how rushed we are as teens to choose a career path and stick to it just to complete the curriculum. Once I completed my education, I began uncovering the things I enjoy doing in my spare time. This had me wishing I could travel back in time to encourage my younger self to focus on the small things that bring me joy. I feel that if I took the time to learn more about myself from the ages 18-now 24, I could have taken my time to really dive into my passions and uncover what it is I am to do in this life."

—Jenna C.

"I want to earn six figures by the age of 30."

—Lara C.

"I hope to become a well-known political analyst and publicist for a variety of organizations."

—Lauren C.

"In 10 years, I strive to be happy in my career, and happy with how far I have come. Too often, college students put so much pressure on themselves, and some may stop and think to say, 'Is this all going to be worth it in the end?' I pray that everything I have worked so hard for during my years in undergrad and during my master's degree, I can look back and say that everything worked out the way it was supposed to and that I truly enjoy the work that I am pursuing. After two internships at large pharmaceutical companies, my professional goal is to help people gain access to medicine, specifically rare disease medications that save lives."

—Margaret C.

"In 10 years, I want to feel stable overall. I think stability is generally something everyone my age longs for, because the process of college and the early stages of our careers comes with so many choices, paths, and 'what ifs.' After all of that, I hope that, in 10 years, it will have paid off in the sense of being able to relax, knowing I've found my footing, both personally and professionally. I've experienced so much change so quickly, that I feel like a sailor in a storm, hoping for smooth waters ahead."

—Ashley D.

"I hope to inspire change, whether in my personal, professional life, or both, and continue to use communication to do good."

—Jenna D.

"To be married, have a strong work/life balance, and feel fulfilled with the work I am doing."

—Jennifer D.

"The next 10 years are going to be big. I want to see myself married with children and happy at home and at work. I've always dreamt of a happy family and although many people are scared to bring kids into the world these days, I'm confident that we can turn our world around. I chose the public relations field so I could help make a difference in communities and I'd love to have a number of campaigns under my belt that showcase social good and community and that make the world better for our kids."

—Joelle D.

"In the next 10 years I hope to rejoin the workforce once my daughters begin school or grow my business enough to provide my daughters an example of a woman-owned business that started in their garage. A dream of mine is that the country can come back together and be untied similar to when I was a child. The world has become a scary place and I want that to change for my children. I do not want my children to have to worry about school shootings, bomb threats and being scared to walk alone because they are women. Something about myself and Gen Z as a whole, is that I believe many of us do not only have dreams and aspirations for ourselves, but we have them for our world, country, community and sub-groups within communities. We want better for ourselves and for generations to come."

—Summer D.

"I hope to find myself in a position that is more focused on ensuring people management and employee development is successful, as that area of a business is the most exciting to me and is necessary to a company that is looking to grow and succeed."

—Troy D.

"In the next 10 years, I hope to turn my afterwork passion, songwriting, singing and music, into a full-time career."

—Cristina F.

"Over the next decade, I want to push myself both physically and mentally to become the best version of myself. Each day, I want to challenge myself and learn something new. I want to travel, meet new people, try new foods and adopt new skills. Most importantly, I want to be sure to live in the moment each and every day growing from my choices and learning from my mistakes. Tomorrow is never promised."

—Gabrielle F.

"In the next 10 years, I hope to achieve professional growth in the advertising/public relations industry. Continuing to work in an agency, potentially as an account lead or director with large or well-known clients."

—Olivia F.

"I hope I can become successful enough to live where I want to comfortably, rise up the ranks in my profession enough to hopefully become a chief marketing officer or a director of sorts, have my family continue to be healthy and happy, and to continue to maintain valuable relationships while fostering new ones in the pursuit for new experiences and realities."

—Adam G.

"In the next ten years I hope to begin building my own family. I'm hopeful that equilibrium will return and things like becoming a homeowner becomes a more realistic economic goal. I choose to be hopeful about our future as a generation because I know that we have every tool imaginable to connect and collaborate – making a bigger table with more seats for all."

—Katie G.

"I try to live my life with as little stress as possible. If I can minimize negativity around me, while having and maintaining the willingness to stay open minded, I can achieve my goals and aspirations. My goals relate to both personal and career growth. I'd like to continue building my value in the sports and entertainment industry while taking risks that present opportunities for higher wages, further savings, and more responsibility. I envision myself owning a home, managing others, answering to equals rather than superiors, and above all else, I want to be happy, healthy, and secure both emotionally and financially."

—Paris G.

"In the next ten years of my professional career, I hope to of course be successful but also make an impact on the issues I care about and work on. It will be important for me to not just get a paycheck, but to feel I am doing meaningful work."

—Pat G.

"Over the next decade I hope to help in the creation of campaigns that really resonate with its target audience. I love seeing how different brands have used social media to engage with its audience, such as Euphoria developing an Apple music playlist and Scrub Daddy commenting on a TikTok video of two kids jokingly singing an original song about scrubbing the dishes, giving them an opportunity to record and release the song."

—Alessandra I.

"I hope to obtain as much knowledge and applicable skills as possible in the first years of my career regarding operating procedures, sanitation, and food safety in multiple environments in the food industry. Utilizing my experience, I eventually want to be able to work for a consulting firm that focuses on food safety. In a world with a growing population, climate change, and currently a pandemic, we are going to have to find innovative solutions to feed the public safely, so I think this field is going to grow in the years to come with a lot of opportunities."

—Ryan J.

"*Professionally, I would love to work in advertising, marketing, or brand management for a large brand. As of now, I only have agency experience, but working on the corporate side for a company such as Adidas, Starbucks, or any other large-scale brand is the goal for my thirties. I would also love to work in marketing within live theater or Broadway purely because of my passion for those things. Personally, I want to be able to travel as much as I can, and I want to own my own home. I had a less than fortunate upbringing, so having a safe place to call home and the ability to see the world are two things that are really important to me.*"

—Gillian K.

"*My goals and aspirations over the next decade (I'll be 32!) are to first graduate college this May, find a full-time job somewhere I enjoy, move up in the company, travel the world (hopefully if Covid allows), find love and settle down eventually, get my own black-lab dog, have kids, and purchase a home! I don't believe in having a strict life plan and I think other people in Gen Z agree, but I do believe in having future goals to look forward to.*"

—Hannah K.

"*Over the next 10 years, I hope to be the greatest version of myself— mentally, physically, financially.*"

—Kayla L.

"In the next 10 years, I hope to be financially stable and able to take care of my family, as well as working within my dream career."

—Kymani L.

"I'm shooting for a VP equivalent level within the next decade. Perhaps I have a chip on my shoulder being a communication major... but I aim to leverage my skill set to continue to be a recognized as a valuable voice."

—Micah L.

"In the next 10 years, I aspire to live a lifestyle where I feel like I have a great work life balance but still hold a high position in the company I choose to be at. I have high goals for my career, but the pandemic has taught me how much I value time with friends and family, so I hope to find a perfect balance of career focus."

—Rachel L.

"I have always imagined myself living out my fashion dreams in my 20s, either working for a big name or starting my own brand. As much as I value my career and making a name for myself, my number one value will always be family. I hope to find my person and start having kids in the next 10 years."

—Hanalee M.

"I hope to achieve my place in healthcare communications to do my best to help others, in a setting that isn't necessarily hands on."

—Matilda M.

"Personally, my goal is to be happy and to travel and explore the world! Professionally, I hope to work in-house in public relations and excel at the job. I hope to continually be learning new things, working on brands that I love and mentoring members of the next generation of PR pros."

—Sarah M.

"In the next 10 years I hope to be happy. Professionally, I hope to be several promotions down the line, and possibly leading my own team. These promotions would of course come with several pay increases, as I would love to be comfortable and financially stable in 10 years—something that seems almost impossible in today's society. Personally, I hope in 10 years I have found the love of my life and we have settled down and started a family."

—Julianna N.

"Over the next ten years I hope to be a change-maker in the sports marketing space by fostering positive change and creating social impact through sports. In addition, I aspire to create my own public relations/marketing firm that represents sports organizations that have meaningful missions and believe in the power of sports."

—Frankie P.

"I hope to continue my work in the Gen Z marketing space and help it become common knowledge that Gen Zers value authentic purpose in the companies they work for and buy from."

—Michael P.

"I really want to act in a big movie or TV show. A few years ago, that would have just stayed a dream. But thanks to graduating right into a pandemic, I got the guts to go freelance and pursue multiple professions, one of which is my dream. I'm auditioning like crazy and booking a few really good gigs, so, the possibility of acting in a big-name project that everyone will have heard of seems to get closer to reality every day. Fingers crossed!"

—Sarah P.

"Over the next 10 years, I aspire to be a leader in my field and work across the entertainment landscape in a variety of facets while creating and having experiences, both personal and professional, that lead me to live and work abroad as I work to bring diversity and social impact to my family and career."

—Alyssa R.

"In ten years, I want to be at a successful music company that provides me with a wide variety of benefits (i.e. health, education, diversity & inclusion, fair pay), a company that gives back to the community, and a company that fights to stop climate change."

—Flor R.

"Over the next decade I would like to complete my master's degree, thankfully I'm only 6 credits away from meeting that goal. I would also like to buy my first home and invest in rental properties."

—Kylie R.

"In the next 10 years, I hope to become a homeowner."

—Roya R.

"I don't have a 10-year-plan because I don't know who I'll be in 10 years. I hope to live a rich life — not by wealth — but a life rich in purpose, experiences, and aspirations for the next 10 years to look forward to, surrounded by those who inspire me to chase my wildest dreams."

—Shelby R.

"Within the next decade, I hope to make a difference in the lives of others and complete work that matters."

—Sydney R.

"I will be a teacher or professor helping students find their dream jobs in five years."

—Geno S.

"I'm not sure what the future holds but I know it'll be bright if I keep following the things I enjoy doing. We're always meeting new people who can change the trajectory of our lives at any time. Over next 10 years, I'm going to continue to say 'yes' to every opportunity that comes my way, be curious, and always open to building new relationships."

—Hailley S.

"In the next decade I hope to earn a master's degree in global sports business."

—Isaiah S.

"I want to feel complete, happy, and like my time has mattered. Whether through my writing or personal life, I am hoping to find my stride, then help others. I want justice, strength, and a peace of mind. Hopefully, if the world can recover from this, I'd also prefer just normalcy again—but until then, I will try my hardest to leave the world better than when I came into it."

—Rebekah S.

"Professionally, I hope to be working in-house somewhere in the next 10 years, preferably in the sports industry."

—Ryan S.

"Over the next 10 years, some of my dreams include completing my master's degree program, securing a great paying job that I love, and to hopefully settle down and raise a healthy family."

—Samantha S.

"I look forward to one day being able to do what I love for a living. That could include working with a music or travel company where I see representation all around me from junior staff to the highest levels."

—Isabeau T.

"Over the next 10 years, I see myself being the best version of myself. I want to do the unexpected and be in a position that I created for myself. Nothing is impossible."

—Rachel U.

"Professionally, I would love to work in sports, but I also would love to use my entrepreneurial side to make a change in the world regarding mental health/anxiety disorder awareness!"

—David W.

"I wish to be in a position where I can help others grow their career. I would not be where I am today without the support I have received from my mentors and will not be able to continue to grow without their future support. To one day be in the position where I can return the favor to my mentors or to those looking to break through whatever industry I am leading is something that I strive for."

—Nicole W.

"My aspiration in the next ten years is to fully integrate myself into the marketing ecosystem. I am passionate to become a marketer who can grow brand awareness through its channels and run campaigns with partnerships. Not only am I passionate about marketing, but I want to utilize it in a way that would better our society. I would love to work with a company, agency, or organization guided by sustainable marketing. I know that the possibilities are endless for me, and I am excited about the journey. My love for the game of golf will not end. I want to continue to succeed at competing at the amateur level. In the next ten years, I want to qualify for the US Amateur Tournament. Playing golf competitively is important to me, and I aspire to integrate it into my life, even when my career starts."

Oliver W.

"I just want to be comfortable. I have reasonable goals. I want to continue my relationship, get married, travel the world, buy a house, meet people and hear their stories, and make a life of experience. Notice how I didn't mention work. I like my job, but I will always prioritize my life over work. I want to advance in my career and eventually join an industry in my field that I love, but in the end, I'm working to live, not living to work. I also want to point out that I am not looking to have children. I think that's becoming increasingly common among young people because of how expensive it is. I want to retire young and having a kid in this world really derails that."

—Nicholas Y.

Final Thoughts

Are you inspired? Are you energized? Are you informed about Generation Z?

If I authored this book correctly, you should be. Each and every time I meet with Gen Zers one-on-one or in a classroom or group setting, I am inspired and energized by their entrepreneurial mindset, their innovative approach, their purposeful intentions and the way in which I see them transforming media, marketing, the workplace and so much more. As I write this, it is only 2022. If you have not yet jumped on the Gen Z bandwagon, you still have time.

Over the next 10-15 years, I believe Gen Z will become the primary consumer segment focus for most organizations, large and small. They will force employers to transform and marketers to innovate or suffer the consequences. Now is the time to immerse yourself in Gen Z in the same manner that I did starting in 2017. Now is the time to embrace this generation and connect and collaborate with them the same way Target started to do with their Gen Z incubator in 2018.

Now is the time to begin to act like Gen Z and become more purposeful in your intentions, more innovative in your thinking and more transformative in your actions. If you do, you will achieve the goals you set and the dreams you only imagined just like the oldest members of Generation Z featured in this book.

About The Author

Mark Beal is one of the nation's leading experts on Generation Z. Beal is an assistant professor of practice in the School of Communication and Information at Rutgers University where he advises the student-run public relations and social media agency. Beal has an MA in Journalism and Mass Communication with a concentration in Public Relations.

Beal served as a public relations practitioner and marketer for more than 25 years, developing and executing public relations campaigns for category leading companies and brands around such major sports and entertainment platforms as the Olympic Games, Super Bowl, World Series, NCAA March Madness, US Open Tennis and The Rolling Stones.

Beal has authored five books include *Decoding Gen Z* and *Engaging Gen Z*. Beal's ongoing research of Gen Z has led to keynote speeches with the American Marketing Association, Association of National Advertisers as well as corporations, brands, sports leagues conferences and agencies. To learn more about Mark, please visit www.markbealspeaks.com

Made in the USA
Columbia, SC
15 September 2022

67239151R00109